To Jonny, my beloved constant,
and Ellen and Aaron, who light my soul.

Contents

Part II—DO: Creating Community

Part III—SHARE: Personal Stories

Note to the Reader

I am a survivor of sexual assault. It was not my fault.

Those two sentences are still, today, a bit uncomfortable to declare. We are conditioned to keep silent and blame ourselves.

But what happens when we no longer keep silent, when we stop blaming ourselves?

We heal. That's what happens.

This book is based upon more than thirty-five years of actively healing from sexual assaults—a healing sojourn that included many, many other survivors. We are numerous. We are connected. Other survivors saved my life and helped me end my isolation. We heal together, not alone.

We never completely get over a sexual assault. It's always with us.

However, when given the opportunity, we can learn how to live beyond surviving. When given the opportunity, we can learn how to intentionally heal, become hopeful, and become empowered. This book will help you do all three.

This is your given opportunity.

Healing from a sexual assault—any type of sexual assault—is not a tidy, linear process. It's not a matter of completing one phase, moving on to the next, and so forth until we've completed every phase and we're "all better." Oh, if it were only that simple!

Rather, healing from sexual assault is a personal journey to rediscover who we truly are, to reclaim what was taken from us, to stand tall without shame and without self-blame, and to feel safe again. That is the journey.

As with any journey, the most difficult part is getting started. So allow this book to serve as your starting point.

Before we begin, let's clarify some basic terminology:

- Throughout the book I use the term *sexual assault*, which is defined by the Rape, Abuse & Incest National Network as "sexual contact or behavior that occurs without explicit consent of the victim." This includes any form of nonconsensual sexual contact or behavior perpetrated against an adult. It also includes *any* form of sexual contact or behavior perpetrated against a child or teenager—because a child cannot consent to sexual activity, period.

- When I refer to *sexual assault survivors*, I'm referring to all humans of any age, gender, orientation, race, or religion who have experienced sexual assault.
- I use *we* throughout the book to provide a sense of oneness, to deliberately break our isolation. We heal together.

This book has three parts, which encompass a survivor's healing journey of BE, DO, and SHARE.

Part I is "BE—Moving Beyond Surviving." It contains five steps that moved me and other survivors forward on our healing journey. The steps are suggestions, not rules to be followed. We are provided an opportunity to go within and get curious about what holds us back from our true BEing.

Each chapter ends with a Gratitude Statement and a simple New Practice exercise. We can't heal without gratitude. We can't heal unless we make some changes. Use what is provided, or create your own.

Part II is "DO—Creating Community." It sets forth guidelines for how to create a healing, safe, and supportive community. What needs to be in place to support the BEing? What do you need to DO to assure the journey continues? Consider it a road map.

Again, we heal together. When we create and participate in a healing community, we belong. When we belong, we cannot be alone.

The guidelines in the "Creating Community" section are not original, nor are they unique. They are based upon personal experiences of belonging to groups that are safe places for healing—and those that are not. I have taken what works and turned that into simple guidelines for creating a sustainable healing community in which we can thrive.

Part III is "SHARE—Personal Stories." It sets forth personal stories written by sexual assault survivors. The stories focus on each survivor's healing journey. This journey never ends, but these stories contain the resilience, hope, and empowerment we wish to pass along to the reader. We SHARE so others can join us, belong, and find freedom.

This book is meant to complement and work in tandem with your existing healing practices. Read this book many times. Read it alone. Read it with other trusted survivors in your community. Each time you read it, it will present an opportunity to shift and change, an opportunity to identify with and find similarities within the text. The goal is to *be*, *do*, and *share* over and over again.

Now it's up to you. Commence your journey through the pages of *Out of the Basement*. Experience what's possible when we shift beyond surviving and into a lifestyle of healing, hope, and empowerment. Create your community of healing.

BE.

DO.

SHARE.

Over and over again.

—Deborah K. Halvorson

The soul that is within me no man can degrade.

—Frederick Douglass

PART I

BE: Moving Beyond Surviving

Step 1

We acknowledge we were sexually assaulted
and that it was not our fault.

Many of us deny our sexual assault even happened. Some of us deny it for many years.

Or if we don't deny it, we minimize it and call it "that thing that happened to me." We certainly do not call it a sexual assault. That would make it real, something serious—a crime, actually. Which it is.

So what happens when we acknowledge we were sexually assaulted? Reality happens. It all becomes real. We can no longer pretend.

And then we are left with the truth: *we were sexually assaulted.*

It's nearly impossible to capture the full impact of that acknowledgment. It's like coming out of a confining space of darkness and stepping into the light.

To Acknowledge

Our denial of our sexual assault is like living in a dark, damp basement. It's not so bad, really. We've adapted and built our life around the dark and the damp. Some of us would even say we're happy down there. We work. We function. We have relationships.

Yet we all agree there's something missing in the basement. There's an emptiness that we just can't seem to fill. There's a pervasive feeling that something is wrong with us.

In response, we engage in all kinds of escapist, avoidant behavior—our created protections. Yet we still feel the emptiness. It's always with us. This is how we live. This is our "normal."

And then one day we notice the stairs.

How long have we been walking by those stairs—unnoticing? Were they always there? Why didn't we see them before now?

It doesn't matter. We see them now. We are ready to see.

We sense there's something else for us up those stairs. Maybe even something better. Just standing there, at the foot of the stairs, we feel a small piece of our emptiness being filled. This feels new, but at the same time, it feels familiar.

Then we look up. For the first time, we notice a door at the very top of the stairs. A way out, perhaps?

Coming from underneath the door is the warmest, most comforting glow of light. We feel something we haven't felt in a long time: hopeful. We're not even sure what we're hopeful about, exactly. We just feel hopeful.

We think about venturing up the stairs. But fear and isolation keep us in our basement. Deep down inside, we know that leaving our damp, dark basement means acknowledging our sexual assault. It means stepping into the unknown. It means leaving behind the familiar comfort and created "safety" of our basement and our protections. We convince ourselves that the emotional pain would be too great—it would surely kill us.

So we turn away from the stairs, receding and retreating into the darkness again.

However, we find ourselves returning to the foot of the stairs from time to time. We keep looking up at the light glowing under the door, and we keep feeling that hopeful feeling.

But we're still uncertain. What should we do? Once again, we don't move.

Then one day we meet—or read about or hear about—a sexual assault survivor who has actually left their basement and ventured up the stairs. They acknowledge their sexual assault. They speak about it without shame or self-blame. They are big and powerful when they speak. They are unafraid.

They are safe outside of their basement.

For the first time we understand our basement—our emptiness. We realize we are not alone. We want what they have. They give us courage.

So, we make our way to the stairs once again. We look up. This time we are ready to move. We lift our feet and take that first step.

It *doesn't* kill us.

This is a huge realization. Leaving the basement may be uncomfortable and scary, yes. But it won't kill us. We can bear it. There's an unknown reserve of strength within us.

We can do this.

So we begin our journey up the stairs. With each step, we keep climbing. It's still scary; we've never done this before. But we keep going.

Then we reach the door. From down in the basement, we could see little more than a hint of the light. Up here, we can see the light in its full power, glowing underneath the door.

We touch the doorknob.

We think maybe we're ready to open the door. We know what's on the other side: hope, acknowledgment, and truth.

Something is giving us the strength to keep going. It's coming from the light but also from within. This is the strength that got us up the stairs—the strength we didn't even know we had.

We feel—perhaps for the first time in a very, very long time—our true feelings and emotions.

They're painful and frightening. But at the same time, there's a powerful feeling that all will be OK.

That *we* are OK. We feel hopeful. We feel safe.

But it's difficult to trust that this will last. It's difficult to trust that anything safe will last.

So we turn around and look down the stairs. The urge to run back down into our damp, dark basement is strong. It's comfortable down there. Familiar.

But then we realize that the hopeful feeling is familiar, too, though just in a different way.

This familiar feeling is one we haven't experienced in a very long time. It's almost like *remembering*. Remembering who we are. Remembering the source of our own strength.

The basement, on the other hand—it's what we *know*. We've been down there for so long.

Then it hits us—what about all that stuff we left behind in the basement? What about our protections? Don't we need those to survive outside the basement?

We start to panic.

Instantly, a sensation comes up from deep inside. It's strong and comforting. It assures us that the basement and its protections no longer fit us. The more we remember the story of the sexual assault survivor who went before us, the more courageous we'll feel.

So we stay at the top of the stairs.

We know *this* is where we need to be right now.

We stand here in this hopeful place, waiting until we receive clarity on what comes next.

Maybe that means we'll stand here for an hour. A day. A month. A year.

It doesn't matter.

We're out of the basement.

We acknowledge we were sexually assaulted.

Not everything that is faced can be changed;
but nothing can be changed until it is faced.

—JAMES BALDWIN

The Truth

To acknowledge we've been sexually assaulted means telling ourselves the truth about what happened to us. It's an unwanted truth, but a truth just the same. And any possibility of joy requires an acknowledgment of this truth, the reality that we were sexually assaulted. This is the only place from which we can begin our journey toward change. We cannot move forward until we see the truth in front of us and then step into it.

So we now have the choice: we can continue moving forward by opening the door and seeing the truth, even though it's very scary, or we can return to the damp, dark basement and our familiar emptiness.

We always have a choice.

In this moment, some of us need to return to the basement for a while. The acknowledgment of the raw truth that we were sexually assaulted seems too overwhelming.

It's very understandable. At least in the basement, we know how to function. Down there, we can hide behind our created protections—the results of our escapist behavior. Silence, denial, and minimizing are familiar, even though they're also oppressive, keeping us empty and stuck.

We must not judge one another for this retreat back to the basement. Our journeys are not all the same. What works for one may not work for another.

However, those who choose to return will soon realize that the basement no longer provides the solace they seek. That's because something happens the instant we speak our truth—the instant we acknowledge we've been sexually assaulted. We cannot unsay it. We cannot un-acknowledge it.

The truth is that powerful.

Once the truth has been revealed, we begin to understand that silence, denial, and minimizing only reinforce our isolation and reinforcc the feeling that something is wrong with us.

We begin to understand that as long as we keep

secrets and suppress the truth, we will remain fundamentally at war with ourselves.

We begin to understand that when we deny or minimize the sexual assault—the truth—we send ourselves the harsh message that we're not worth it. That we're not important enough to be believed and treated with kindness. That we're just not *enough*.

Finally, we begin to understand that when we hide from our sexual assault or dismiss it, we lose our chance to break free from the chains that keep us stuck in the past. We realize that denial of the truth steals our opportunity to bring forth our inherent inner strength and power. Denial allows the sexual assault to win.

Relief only comes when we make our way back to the hopeful place at the top of the stairs to acknowledge the sexual assault. The truth causes the assault to lose its raw power to frighten us. We no longer need to fight against it.

Instead, we work *with* it.

So we push open the door at the top of the stairs and feel the power, strength, and hope of the truth.

Three things that cannot be long hidden:
the sun, the moon, and the truth.

—BUDDHA

STEP 1

It Was Not Our Fault

We must never, ever underestimate the tremendous courage it takes to climb out of the basement and acknowledge that we were sexually assaulted.

It takes even more courage to also acknowledge that *it was not our fault.*

That's because we live in a culture that readily denies sexual assault. We are actually conditioned to lie about it and conditioned to believe it was our fault. To deceive ourselves. To hide in the basement, away from any possible hope that life could be different.

Down there, we deny the assault happened. We minimize its severity and effects on our emotional development. And we make it our fault.

What causes us to do this? How can we say such an overt act of violence never happened? How can we say it wasn't *that* big of a deal?

Worst of all, how can we blame ourselves for it?

Numerous neurological and psychological research articles and books have been written about the human response to trauma and why we blame ourselves. Our self-blame is actually quite a normal response to a very abnormal situation. We could all benefit from exploring this extremely useful and helpful information with a trusted therapist or a trusted survivor.

To keep it simple for the purposes of this book,

our self-blaming response is for survival.

The betrayal of a sexual assault cuts deeper into our heart and soul than any other. When our favorite aunt or uncle assaults us; when our cousin or neighbor assaults us; when the trusted priest or pastor or rabbi or imam assaults us; when our beloved parent assaults us; when our doctor, teacher, or coach assaults us; when someone we thought was a friend assaults us; when our first date with that great person ends in an assault; when we are assaulted walking to our car; when we are repeatedly assaulted as a child or a spouse or partner—WHO CAN MAKE SENSE OF THIS?

The immense betrayal shocks our system. It's beyond our capacity to take in.

Quite simply, it's easier for our brains to come up with an explanation, a reason, something to blame. And sadly, for most of us, that explanation, reason, and blame rest with ourselves.

Or so we think.

We come up with subtle ways to blame ourselves for the sexual assault. Rather than reacting with total outrage toward the person who committed the assault—the perpetrator—we focus on what *we* did or did not do, which is just another way to blame ourselves. We think it's the only way to make sense of an incomprehensible act of violence.

Let's be very clear: *any* sexual assault is an act of violence, no matter the circumstances or situation.

But because it's nearly impossible to understand why such violence has been perpetrated against us, unprovoked, through no fault of our own, it seems logical to assume the fault must somehow be ours. Self-blame is how we make sense of violence that makes no sense.

Self-blame is subtle and insidious. It shows up in many sneaky ways. Here are a few:

- "I'm sure they didn't mean it. I must have said/done something to make them think that was OK."
- "They're always goofing around. This time, they accidentally went too far."
- "I wonder what I did to bring that on . . ."
- "What was I thinking, inviting them to my apartment / going to their apartment? What did I expect?"
- "What was I thinking, wearing those clothes? I was asking for it."
- "It never would have happened had I not been drunk. What did I expect?"
- "It wasn't a big deal. These things happen all the time. I just need to move on."
- "I should have yelled or fought back."

- "I should have taken that self-defense class."
- "Why did I walk to my car alone?"
- "Why didn't I keep saying no? I just gave in."

When something so unimaginable happens to us, it's only natural to slip into a mindset of denial, minimizing, and self-blame. Who wouldn't? It's difficult to get beyond the feeling that we must be at least partially to blame.

For those of us who bravely tell someone about the assault, it's common to be met with more denial, minimizing, and blame. Many times, people don't believe us; they shame us.

So, when we need the most compassion, comfort, and care, we are left alone.

We are betrayed again.

There is no greater isolation or loneliness than carrying this burden ourselves. It's like a slow-moving, oily ooze that creeps into every nook and cranny of our being.

It robs us of the feeling that we are in charge of ourselves. It robs us of our personal agency, our confidence, our safety.

So in order to survive, we try to reconcile the assault in some way. We settle on "It was my fault," we make our way into that dark basement, and we adjust our life accordingly.

We build walls in an attempt to protect ourselves

from the slow-moving ooze as well as any potential betrayals or hurts or failures. We shove the sexual assault into the back corner of the basement. We close off that part of ourselves.

The fear of remembering or even acknowledging what's in the back corner is so unbearable that we try to run from it. We become escape artists, running to every other corner of the basement in a futile attempt to get away. We engage in compulsive—sometimes very harmful—behaviors that help us "forget" or that assist us in the art of minimizing. These escapist behaviors make our basement "comfortable."

Our escapist behaviors show up in a variety of different ways:

- We drink too much.
- We smoke too much weed.
- We act out sexually.
- We work to excess.
- We frequently change jobs.
- We overeat.
- We undereat.
- We practice body hate.
- We gamble to excess.

- We shop and buy too much stuff.
- We engage in self-mutilation.
- We are perfectionists who constantly fail.
- We are overachievers who are never satisfied.
- We are people pleasers begging for acceptance and approval.
- We are angry and confrontational.
- We are victims of everything.
- We are the judge of everything and everyone.
- We must control our physical environment to be safe.
- We must control everyone around us to feel safe.

The list goes on ad infinitum. There are many, many ways we try to escape our thoughts, to block out the remembering, the truth.

And so we carry on like this in the basement. Sometimes for years. Most of us confuse this with *living*.

It seems to work for a while—or at least that's what we tell ourselves.

What actually happens, though, is that the sexual assault sits in that corner. It festers and continues to wound us.

Eventually, we reach the inevitable point where our escapist lifestyle actually turns on us. We begin to feel the harming effects of our compulsive and overcompensating behaviors.

No matter how hard we try, we cannot deny one part of our Self and live fully. Nor can we truly live in the basement, away from the truth.

It just doesn't work. It's the escaping, the running away, that perpetuates our burden of loneliness, isolation, and longing. The truth is always trying to get out and be recognized, be acknowledged.

You never find yourself until you face the truth.

—Pearl Bailey

What suffers the most is the relationship with our Self. Most of us are not fully aware of the blow we deliver to our Self each time we take on the shame and self-blame of our sexual assault. With each blow, we become smaller and smaller, less safe, more alone.

We are trying to survive. But there's a strong part within each one of us that wants to move beyond surviving. For many of us, it takes a long time to bring this part of us forward or to even realize it exists within us. And when we do, this is what draws us to the foot of the stairs, where we can look up at the hopeful light glowing under the door. This is what pulls us forward to begin that climb. This is what gives us the courage to open the door to the truth.

Our mantra must become "It was not my fault. It was not my fault."

It is uncomfortable to say, even to ourselves. It will feel like a lie. That's OK.

Nowhere in this step does it say we have to immediately and fully *believe* it was not our fault. That's not a requirement.

All we have to do at this phase of our healing is *acknowledge* it happened and *acknowledge* it was not our fault.

The words come first, then the mind eventually follows. Believing the words is an evolving process that requires patience and kindness toward our Self. Evolution is not a straight line. Sometimes it will feel as though we're not moving at all, and then we'll move.

Allow the evolution.

So let's step away from what we have created as our protective barriers, our protective lifestyle. Let's turn around and look at what's left behind in the basement. The light from the open door allows us to see into each nook, cranny, and corner. What we see no longer frightens us. It's time to learn how to live with the acknowledgment, the truth.

So we step through the door and stand in the light of hope.

So, no matter what the difficulty around you or the darkness before you, turn on the light. No matter what happens, turn on the light and keep it on.

—Eric Butterworth

Gratitude Statement

"With gratitude, I stand with my whole Self in the light at the top of the stairs and speak the truth."

New Practice

Acknowledge to yourself you were sexually assaulted. Tell your story to yourself. Tell your truth. End each truth statement with "It was not my fault."

Step 2

We develop our inherent Spiritual Connection within to move beyond our shame and self-blame and to restore our sense of safety.

As we learn to function outside the basement, many of us engage the services of qualified trauma experts or professionals to help us deal with our acknowledged truth: we were sexually assaulted. Many of us received this expert and professional guidance years ago.

This useful and necessary mental health guidance helps us successfully identify and mitigate the immediate trauma triggers from our sexual assault. This professional help is instrumental in transitioning us out of the basement so we can begin addressing our escape-artist behavior and discover our innate resilience and resourcefulness.

Once these immediate needs have been addressed, many of us believe we're functioning just fine—or as well as can be expected under the circumstances. Not great, but *just fine.*

Yet on some deeper level, we still feel it—the residue.

While there are many residual effects of sexual assault, the most prevalent and seemingly universal effects are shame, self-blame, and what we'll call *never-safe*—no sense of safety.

This residue is familiar but not always easy to identify. It's what makes us want to retreat back into the basement and engage in our protective behaviors.

At this juncture, we must be patient with ourselves. We must understand that simply being out of the basement doesn't mean we've miraculously shed everything we created down there. Sexual assault residue hangs on. It ripples through every aspect of our lives.

For many of us, this residue is so ingrained, so conditioned that we don't even know it's there. We lack the awareness to identify our shame. We don't realize we're blaming ourselves for the violence committed against us. We believe never-safe is an acceptable state of mind that will always be with us.

Others of us are aware of the residue, and we know we should rid ourselves of it—yet awareness and knowing are not enough. When we do think or talk about the assault, we tell ourselves and others that the shame is with the perpetrator, not us—yet we still feel it. We tell ourselves that the assault was not our fault, that we're not to blame—yet we still replay events over and over, thinking how we could have done things differently. We tell ourselves we are safe—yet we're constantly on high alert for danger and harm, especially betrayal.

We try—most of us really, really hard—to make the residue go away. But it's still there. It lingers.

Whether we're consciously aware of the residue or not, we're left feeling like there's something truly wrong with us, to our core. This is perhaps the most damaging falsehood we must overcome.

But how?

We need a deeper level of healing. This level of healing must come from within.

What lies behind you and what lies in front of you, pales in comparison to what lies inside of you.

—Attributed to Ralph Waldo Emerson

Our Inherent Spiritual Connection

It's time to access and develop what is already within each one of us: our inherent *Spiritual Connection*.

"Our *what*?" is the first question most of us ask. The answer is quite simple.

Each of us came into the world with a Spiritual Connection. It's our connection to something greater than ourselves. It's that piece of the Divine, the Great Spirit, the Creator, the Universe, the Source, God—call it whatever you choose—that lives in each of us.

Our inherent Spiritual Connection just *is*. It's what moves us beyond our shame, self-blame, and never-safe emotions. It's our inner source of strength, courage, resilience, resourcefulness, and goodness. Our own divinity.

Our Spiritual Connection is what brought us to the basement stairs. It's the source of the courage and strength necessary to climb the stairs, open the door, and step into the light—the truth. It is within each one of us.

Our Spiritual Connection is the part of us that cannot be hurt, no matter what happens to us. It's our undamaged Self. The part of us that knows, deep down, we are not what happened to us. The part of us that knows we are so much more.

Our Spiritual Connection speaks the truth we've forgotten: that we have always been and will always be strong, courageous, and full of goodness. It's the truth we've always known at some deeper level.

Accessing and developing our Spiritual Connection is not about *adding* anything. It's about *finding* what is already there. What has always been there. Since the day we were born. It's a part of us like the ocean is in the wave. Like the snow is in the snowflake. Like the rain is in the raindrop. You cannot have one without the other.

There is a force in the universe, which, if we permit it, will flow through us and produce miraculous results.

—Gandhi

If we're honest, deep down within each one of us is the fundamental belief of something greater than ourselves. We are connected to that Something Greater. For many of us, this fundamental belief has been dormant for years.

Some of us have doubted it or even rebelled against it.

Some of us associate any talk of Spiritual Connection with organized religion. This association can be negative for some of us.

Many of us have been abused by religious leaders. We consider any discussion of a Spiritual Connection to be tainted and false.

Others of us have given very little thought to anything spiritual of any kind. We have little or no use for it.

Others of us have been introduced to the concept of something greater than ourselves, yet we can't fathom the notion of the Divine *within* us. We feel it's too abstract, too egocentric, too radical, too contrary to our religious teachings and traditions.

And then nearly all of us ask perhaps the most challenging question of all: *Why didn't our Spiritual Connection or this Something Greater, if it exists at all, rescue us from this horrific and tragic assault?*

That's a fair question, indeed.

Many of us believe we were left behind—alone, forsaken—at a time when we really could have used some sort of god or divinity or something greater to rescue us. If we're to believe in this Spiritual Connection business, it seems fair to ask, *Shouldn't it have saved us?*

The harsh reality is no.

There is no saving. No stopping bad things from happening. There is no magic wand to wave and no "right" path to walk that will shield us from the human experience that inevitably includes pain.

As humans, we get to choose and experience how we want to live our lives and how we want to treat one another. Some people choose to perpetrate horrific and tragic crimes against others. Horrible things happen to good, decent people every single day. This has been happening since humans first walked the earth.

We can't stop others from making horrible, harmful choices. But we can stop blaming ourselves for other people's choices. We can stop taking on *their* shame. We can take back our safety.

The blame belongs to the perpetrator of the assault. The shame belongs to the perpetrator of the assault. Our stolen safety is because of the perpetrator of the assault. *All* of the lingering residue belongs to the perpetrator. None of it belongs to us, yet we carry it.

So, how do we stop carrying the shame, the self-blame? How do we take back our safety?

The answer is very simple: bring forth our inherent Spiritual Connection. Our divinity within. This is our source of strength, courage, resilience, resourcefulness, and goodness. It's what keeps us moving, evolving. It's our solid foundation.

We've all felt it, experienced it—that connection. But perhaps we lacked the awareness to recognize it. It shows up as the light glowing under the basement door at the top of the stairs, the light in and around us as we open the door. It shows up as the courage to see and speak the truth. It shows up as our ability to see the goodness in ourselves and others.

It's always been there, even at our most difficult moments, holding our strength, goodness, and healing power.

Our Spiritual Connection reminds us that we are never forsaken. Never alone. It's time to bring it forth.

If you bring forth what is within you,
what you bring forth will save you.

—Gospel of Thomas 70

Connection to Others

Our Spiritual Connection ties us to others as well. If we spend time with trusted sexual assault survivors who seem to no longer struggle in the same way we do, we can witness our first signs that this transformative power exists within.

In these survivors' stories, we hear their courage and strength. We hear about their ability to move forward and stand tall. We hear how they developed their inherent Spiritual Connection, which then allowed them to move beyond the residue of the assault. Developing their Spiritual Connection allowed them to save themselves *from within.*

We learn from the wisdom of those who have gone before us. As a result, we begin to understand and believe in our own healing power.

Together, we can identify and understand these plaguing, residual emotions that get into every nook and cranny of our being. We begin to understand and identify our deep-seated shame, our pervasive and subtle self-blame, and our never-safe feelings that manifest as distrust of everyone and everything.

We can teach one another to move forward. There's a powerful energy when we come together to heal and connect with the Divine Source uniting us all.

But to access this energy, we have to actively

choose to come together—just as we have to actively choose to bring forth our Spiritual Connection. It's not a passive process; it's a choice.

A fork in the road.

Everything you need to make it through the most painful, difficult, and challenging issues of your life exists within you. Do not under any circumstances doubt your power!

—Iyanla Vanzant

Pick Your Pain

We all arrive at this fork. This choice. Some of us more than once.

To the left is the familiar path of life as we know it, functioning *just fine* in the residue.

To the right is the unfamiliar path of Spiritual Connection that offers joy and freedom.

Let's be honest: both paths are painful.

The pain on the path to the left is familiar. It's that *just fine* place with our protective escapist behaviors. It's comfortable discomfort. We know how to function with the residue.

But it's cyclical. It keeps going around and around, like the little hamster running on its wheel, never getting anywhere, never allowing us to be free of shame, self-blame, and never-safe. Painful.

The pain on the path to the right is fear: fear of the unknown, fear of hope, fear of failure, fear of trust, fear of surrender—and ultimately a fear of joy and freedom. But this pain is temporary. That's because fear loses its power the moment we choose to step into it instead of running away from it. But stepping into our fear—allowing it—is unfamiliar, uncomfortable, seemingly impossible. Painful.

We have arrived at the pick-your-pain moment. Many of us hesitate here.

You gain strength, courage, and confidence
by every experience in which you really stop
to look fear in the face. . . . You must do the thing
you think you cannot do.

—Eleanor Roosevelt

Throughout our healing journey, we will be faced with many forks in the road and many pick-your-pain choices such as this. The intentional act of choosing is the most important part of this process.

We always get to choose. For that matter, we always get to change our mind. We can begin down one path, then turn around at any time and choose the other. Both paths are always there. Our healing journeys are not linear.

So, which path will you choose today, at

this moment?

To keep this simple, let's ask: *How's life working for me right now? Am I joyous and free?*

At first, we may be tempted to give our typical answer: *I'm just fine.*

We may also hear the loud and familiar negative self-talk voice: *Quit whining! Everyone has something. This is your something. Big deal. Quit feeling sorry for yourself! Look at all the good things you have. You should be grateful!*

Indeed, nearly all of us can point to good things in our life for which we feel grateful. However, those good things do not cancel out the isolating burden of shame, self-blame, and never-safe.

So, ask yourself again: *How's life working for me right now? Am I joyous and free? Am I?*

For most of us, the honest answer is no.

No, I'm not joyous and free. I don't even know what that means. I'm stuck. I keep thinking about what happened. I'm still running from it. I'm minimizing and pretending it's no big deal. I'm a perfectionist who is constantly not good enough. I'm a people pleaser begging for acceptance and approval. I judge myself and others all the time. I want this feeling—whatever it is—to go away. But no matter what I do, it lingers, it remains.

It's OK. That's all of us at some point. That's shame, self-blame, and never-safe at work.

But right now, we have the opportunity to intentionally choose a different life. A different path.

We can choose the path to the left—choose to stay *just fine*; choose to carry the residue of shame, self-blame, and never-safe; choose to keep doing everything the same. Remain stuck.

Or we can choose the path to the right—choose to face our fear, choose to move beyond the residue, and choose to work toward joyous and free.

One path continues the pain; the other goes through the pain. It's a choice.

I shall be telling this with a sigh
Somewhere ages and ages hence:
Two roads diverged in a wood, and I—
I took the one less traveled by,
And that has made all the difference.

—Robert Frost

Trust and Surrender

To take this path to the right, to go through the pain, all we have to do is trust in our inherent Spiritual Connection within and surrender to its transformative power.

Oh, is that all? we ask sarcastically.

Boy, that's a tough one, isn't it?

Trust and surrender don't come easily to most people. They certainly don't come easily to sexual assault survivors.

For many of us, the words *trust* and *surrender* make us want to slam this book shut and dive into any one of our many protective behaviors.

We trust no *one!* we collectively shout. *We do* not *surrender!*

We are tough and strong. We have to be. That's because we've been let down and betrayed by people we trusted—usually by people who were supposed to care for us and keep us safe.

Trust and surrender make us weak and vulnerable and unsafe! we exclaim. *Yet now we're supposed to trust in and surrender to some Spiritual Connection, some divinity within?!*

Again, we may want to slam the book shut at this point, but let's take a deep breath and keep reading! This book does not promise to have answers for everyone, but it does provide answers and solutions for many of us.

And one of the solutions is to redefine *trust* and *surrender* in new ways so we can call upon our powerful Spiritual Connection to bring forth what's already within us: our existing reserve of strength, courage, and kindness that will guide us through the pain and lead us to healing.

We can define *surrender* as asking our Spiritual Connection for help, and *trust* as choosing to believe that our request will be answered. It's that simple.

Ironically, most of us are more than willing to

lend a helping hand to someone else in need, yet we struggle with asking for help ourselves. That's because society puts distorted importance on "going it alone." In fact, many of us feel a certain amount of pride in handling our troubles by ourselves.

This is my burden, and I must carry it alone, we declare. *I can handle it.*

We call this independence.

It's actually isolation.

Both trust and surrender require vulnerability, yes. But it's not about weakness or submission. It's about strength, courage, and kindness. There is immense, vulnerable strength in asking for help. And it's not about placing ourselves in harm's way or risking our safety; it's about courageously doing something different. When we ask for help, we are responding differently, which allows for the creation of different solutions. When *we're* different, everything is different.

We can choose to believe that there is, in fact, something greater and deeper within us, waiting to be brought forth. Something we *can* trust in and surrender to.

All we need is to be willing to take that first step.

Life begins at the end of your comfort zone.

—NEALE DONALD WALSCH

Willingness

How we walk this new, unfamiliar path through our pain isn't important. All that matters is our willingness to walk it—to be open to our Spiritual Connection, to believe, to trust, to surrender.

So it's time to ask ourselves the questions:

Are we willing to call upon our Spiritual Connection and face the shame, self-blame, and never-safe feelings?

Are we willing to trust in and surrender to a divine force that's ready to walk with us into the pain, the healing, and help us come out on the other side, joyous and free?

Are we willing to believe in something we cannot see yet deeply know is there?

Are we willing to keep calling upon this Great Power within, even when it feels like there's nothing there?

Are we willing to say, *We don't know how to do this, but we're willing to learn?*

Are we willing to shift from *Why did this happen to me?* into *How do I move through this?*

Are we willing to live in the jungle for a while?

Are we willing to step out of our comfort zone?

Are we willing to believe it's *possible* to reach a point in our life where we are no longer controlled by shame, self-blame, and never-safe emotions?

Are we willing to believe it's *possible* the Universe

or God or the Great Spirit within can guide us to joy and freedom?

Are we willing to believe it's *possible* this Divine Source wants us to know that first and foremost we are love and goodness?

If we can answer yes to even one of these questions, then we must take that first step—and the next, and the next—to bring forth our Spiritual Connection and walk the path toward joy and freedom.

The way won't be easy. We've carried the residue of sexual assault for so long that it seems impossible to even *consider* being free of shame, self-blame, and never-safe—let alone to *actually be* free of it.

But it's not impossible.

It's an opportunity.

Bringing forth and trusting our Spiritual Connection is an opportunity to respond differently rather than to continuously react. An opportunity to call upon that which is already within us: great courage, strength, and goodness.

It's already there—let us bring it forth.

Let's remember who we really are.

For behold, the Kingdom of God is within you.

—LUKE 17:21 (KJV)

Gratitude Statement

"With gratitude, I bring forth my inherent Spiritual Connection to move me beyond shame, self-blame, and never-safe and to move me into joy and freedom."

New Practice

Intentionally bring forth your Spiritual Connection and notice each opportunity to respond differently—and then do it.

Step 3

Using our Spiritual Connection, we become aware of the conditioned negative and limiting self-beliefs, and we learn to quiet the accompanying negative self-talk.

Our Spiritual Connection to the Divine that lives in all of us provides us with the courage to enter into this next phase of our healing. As we develop our regular, intentional practice of calling forth and tapping into our Spiritual Connection, we also develop a new awareness of how we think and feel about ourselves.

We begin to actually notice and identify when we feel the residual emotions of shame, self-blame, and never-safe. We begin to understand that "something else" is lingering underneath those three emotions . . . though we're not sure what.

We are ready to go deeper. We are ready to uncover the "something else" we sense is there:

the conditioned negative and limiting self-beliefs, which feed the negative self-talk.

Negative and Limiting Self-Beliefs

Why is an entire chapter dedicated to negative and limiting self-beliefs?

Because they rule us.

What are negative and limiting self-beliefs? They are the deep-seated, conditioned beliefs we have about ourselves. They are the burden put upon us by the perpetrator. Many of them are quite harsh, and many have existed within us for a very long time. Most of us have been carrying them around and living with them since we were children. They do not belong to us, but we are conditioned to absorb them, to believe them.

Here are just a few examples of the negative and limiting self-beliefs many of us are up against:

I'm a loser.
I'm unlovable.
I'm stupid.
I'm damaged.
I'm not good enough.
I'm a failure.
I'm not worth it.
I'm bad.
I'm ugly and fat.

Now, here's the tricky part: we don't actually *acknowledge* these belief statements to ourselves. In fact, many of us are consciously unaware they exist within us. Everyone has at least one or two that circle around each time we need to make a big decision or tackle a difficult situation, or when we have conflict with others or we make a mistake. It's the doubt we feel. It's the shame we feel. It's the distrust of ourselves.

Most people can manage the negative self-beliefs, to a certain degree, by focusing on their reinforced positive self-beliefs. It's the yin and yang of life. The balance.

But what happens when a sexual assault explodes into the life mix? What happens when we are raised in homes where sexual assault is a regular occurrence?

We lose our balance. For many of us, there was never a "balance" to lose.

The sexual assault sears negative self-beliefs into our very being. We actually *feel* those belief statements—or at least one or two of them—to our core. We think the sexual assault actually *proves* the truth of the negative self-belief. We *become* the negative self-belief the perpetrator put upon us.

For example, we make statements such as, "I put myself in that situation. It [the sexual assault] never would have happened if I weren't such a loser or so stupid." Or, "Why didn't I yell or fight back? I'm weak." Or, "If they really loved me, they wouldn't do this. I must not be lovable."

The negative self-beliefs feed the self-blame messages—the negative self-talk.

The greatest sources of our suffering
are the lies we tell ourselves.

—ELVIN SEMRAD, AS QUOTED BY
BESSEL A. VAN DER KOLK

Negative Self-Talk

We all know the voice—the negative self-talk. It's the inner judge. It's the committee. It's that constant chatter in our heads. It's the product of the conditioned negative self-beliefs. It's very loud.

Sadly, we get used to the noise. We figure this is just the way it is. We believe this is who we are.

And when we believe it long enough, we no longer hear it—*we feel it to our core*. The negative self-beliefs are reinforced.

When we continually reinforce the negative self-beliefs, we have no balance, nothing to hang on to. We shift our behavior around the lie. We lose who we truly are. We rarely feel safe.

Feeling that sense of never-safe makes us then move into our familiar protective mode. We want to escape the noise. We want to escape *that feeling.*

So we drink too much. We smoke too much weed. We overeat. We undereat. We act out sexually. We try to make everyone else happy but neglect ourselves. We work to excess. We try to control the uncontrollable. We repeatedly expect perfection from ourselves but then end up disappointed. We are anxious and worried and obsessed with our future. We feel victimized and fragile. We damage our relationships. We become depressed . . . The beat goes on.

The negative self-talk and our escapist, protective behavior keep us from remembering and feeling the true impact of the sexual assault.

It can be difficult to actually identify the negative self-talk. That's because it's very familiar. We're used to it—conditioned to believe it. It's also difficult to identify because it seemingly served a purpose in the beginning. It protected us by building what we considered to be walls of safety.

Those walls allowed us to give the outside appearance of control and order in our lives. We believe that when we "control" our environment, no one and nothing can hurt us. We believe we are safe. We believe we can cover up our feelings of not-enough and our lack of self-acceptance and self-love.

This works for a long time—until it doesn't.

As we start to heal, we become painfully aware

that our so-called walls of safety actually keep us isolated. They keep us from freedom, keep us from a deep Spiritual Connection, keep us from healthy relationships, keep us from who we truly are. For many of us, the wall the negative self-talk has created is so big and so tall we can no longer see over the top. Our protection has become our isolation.

We created this protection to keep us "safe" from remembering and feeling. It's a subtle brilliance, actually. We've unconsciously created a way to deflect and distract ourselves from remembering and feeling the horrific sexual assault.

But the unfortunate part of this brilliant creation is that *we turn on ourselves.*

To keep "safe," we distract ourselves with all kinds of lies about who we are. What better way to escape or distract ourselves than to start an internal fight with ourselves? When we're constantly at war, there's no room to think about anything else. We can avoid thinking about or dealing with the sexual assault.

As long as we keep the focus on personal judgment and negative chatter, we reinforce the underlying negative self-beliefs that started it all. As long as we keep hammering away at ourselves, we become blind to our inner resources and capabilities, to our own agency and ability to lessen the impact of the sexual assault.

For many of us, this becomes our way of life. Our normal.

Now what? we ask. *What do we do with all this negative self-belief and self-talk information? How do we stop the noise? Stop that feeling? How do we shift our self-beliefs? How do we function without our protections? Seriously, how do we do that? It's overwhelming!*

Indeed, it seems impossible. But other survivors have gone before us and have paved the way from *impossible* to *possible.*

How have they done this?

By staying in today.

You wanna fly, you got to give up the shit
that weighs you down.

—Toni Morrison

Living in Today

As we uncover the negative and limiting self-beliefs put upon us, it's vital that we practice living in today. Living in today means just that—staying in today, in what's happening right now, in this moment. It means not living in yesterday nor in tomorrow.

If we stay anchored in today, right in this moment, we know the sexual assault happen*ed*. In the past. It is not happening *now*. We are safe.

Living in today also means we stop obsessing about the future, about tomorrow, next week, next month, or even next year. All we have is what's right in front of us now.

Many of us experience varying levels of anxiety, worry, and fear about the past and the future. These emotions are real. However, they can easily turn obsessive. They keep us running on the circular hamster wheel. Playing the same loop over and over in our heads but developing no solutions.

We cannot move forward into freedom as long as we're repeatedly pulled back into the past or fretting about the future. Healing occurs in the present, in the now, today.

OK, you say. *I understand all that, but* how *do we stay in today? What is the practice?*

These are common questions we all ask.

As with any type of healing, there is no one-size-fits-all answer. As we create our own healing, we will develop our own practices that work best for each of us.

For now, to get started, here is a simple practice that has worked for many of us: when we find ourselves anxious or worried or obsessed about our past, or when we find ourselves anxious or worried or obsessed about our future, we *pause*, *breathe*, and *tap into our Spiritual Connection*.

Tapping into the divinity within us allows us

to focus on the strength within us. From this place, we ask ourselves these questions:

What's going on right now? Take the time to actually answer that question.

Where am I? Take the time to look around and describe the current surroundings.

What's safe now? Take the time to define what is safe right now.

What can I do for myself right now? Listen for the answer. It will come quickly. Trust it, then do it.

The answers come from our inner wisdom—our Spiritual Connection. When we pause and intentionally connect with our inner divinity, we become present, we become brave, we create our healing.

Practice this method regularly until the benefits are realized. Living in today is a deliberate, intentional practice. It increases our trust in ourselves and in our Spiritual Connection.

With trust comes a feeling of safety and security. When we feel safe and secure, our anxiety, worry, and obsession fade. We learn to work in tandem with our Spiritual Connection to keep us living in today.

Remember: anxiety, worry, and obsession cannot survive in the present moment.

This practice is vitally important if we wish to jump off the hamster wheel and move into a deeper level of our healing.

The past has no power over the present moment.
—ECKHART TOLLE

Noticing, Acknowledging, and Awareness

By continuing to strengthen our Spiritual Connection and practice staying in today, we receive the ability to see that our shame, self-blame, and never-safe emotions are not only isolating us but controlling us—enforcing the deep-seated negative self-beliefs and feeding the accompanying negative self-talk.

We also receive the ability to see that we've learned to alter our life around these debilitating emotions. We've learned to serve them. To function within their dysfunction.

Instead of addressing the negative messages and emotions head-on, we keep trying to appease them and even escape them. Yet it seems they are always with us. Relentless.

At the same time, from way back in the recesses of our mind, we always—*always*—hear the calm, quiet voice of our inner Spiritual Connection telling us the truth: we are good, we are kind, we are worthy of love, it was not our fault, this is not our shame, we are safe.

Sadly, we easily dismiss those quiet messages because the negative self-talk is louder, more demanding, more familiar, and—let's face it—easier to believe.

So how do we face the negative self-talk head-on? How do we stop the chatter, which leads to our protective escapist behaviors? How do we quiet the negative chatter so we can hear the messages of our Spiritual Connection?

We practice.

We already have, within us, the resources and the capabilities to shut down the negative self-talk and truly get off the hamster wheel. It's hard to believe, but it's true. We are *that* resourceful, capable, and strong.

All we need is to call upon our Spiritual Connection, our true inner strength. When we draw forward the calm, quiet voice within—our Spiritual Connection—it can help us develop a new practice that intentionally notices and acknowledges the negative self-talk *as it is happening*. It helps us learn how to recognize the mental and physical toll of the negative self-talk.

To begin, pay attention and notice how many times in a single day you do the following:

- Question yourself
- Judge others

- Think someone is judging you
- Judge yourself because it (whatever *it* may be) wasn't done correctly or perfectly
- Express dissatisfaction and hate, either aloud or to yourself, about your body
- Seek approval from others by trying to please them
- Overeat or drink to excess or do some other escapist behavior in the hope it'll help you feel better

Acknowledge this as the negative self-talk. Keep breathing.

Next—and this is equally important—*identify the body sensation* that accompanies the negative self-talk. Notice if you feel any of the following:

- A tightness or heaviness in the chest
- A slight knot or nausea in the stomach area
- A stiffness in the neck and shoulders
- An annoying headache or even a migraine
- An overall restless feeling, with a need to escape or run

Many of us are quite surprised, even startled, when we trace these seemingly unrelated body reactions back to the negative self-talk. Breathe into the body sensation.

Noticing and acknowledging the negative self-talk is a practice. And it *takes time*—deliberate, daily. It's like building inner muscles. To make them strong, we must exercise them. Every day.

There's no right or wrong way to practice. Just do it.

Like any strength-training exercise, this practice will be uncomfortable and difficult at first. Throughout, we'll want to find an easier, less uncomfortable practice.

But let's be honest with ourselves . . . We've already tried the easier, less uncomfortable way. It doesn't work.

We all encounter resistance at this phase of our healing. Expect the negative self-talk to rear its head and judge this practice as stupid or unnecessary. It may even subtly whisper, "This doesn't apply to me—it's for those others. But *I'm* managing just fine."

When this happens, we push through. We keep noticing—without judgment. We keep acknowledging—without judgment. We keep feeling whatever it is we're feeling—without judgment. We keep accepting those feelings—without judgment.

Many of us find it helpful to deliberately break the resistance energy by doing a simple physical movement, such as rubbing our arms, clapping, tapping our forehead, or jumping in place. Create your own "resistance move" and then do it.

Patience and kindness toward ourselves are a must. For many of us, that will be a new practice as well. We're not used to treating ourselves that way.

Be aware of the inner Spiritual Connection during this phase. It's vital to our perseverance.

Also be aware of the guidance and support we can receive from other trusted sexual assault survivors. They keep us going. If we wish to believe and trust in this new practice, it's important to witness how others have benefited from it. It's important to see how they have gained an awareness and connection with the Self that, for many of us, has been buried.

With time, this practice allows us to understand, with clarity, the mental and physical strain we have been under. *This is awareness.*

With awareness, change is now possible. With awareness, we have been given the gift of choice.

The things we are attached to are no more than shadows of the past.

—Ilchi Lee

Making Peace

It's very difficult to turn around and challenge the negative self-talk. It's difficult to convince ourselves that the underlying negative self-beliefs are *not* true. We've spent so much time and energy believing the lies.

It's important, then, to remember that we all possess a tremendous level of courage and brilliance; otherwise, we never would have survived this long. Our courage and brilliance allowed us to create a life filled with protections and escape options.

But something needs to change.

Remember: we cannot quiet the negative self-talk and rid ourselves of the limiting self-beliefs unless we challenge the conditioned thinking that formed them in the first place. Our thinking has been hijacked. The negative self-talk and limiting self-beliefs are not *ours*. We need to reclaim our true voice and our true thoughts.

We must teach ourselves to *respond* rather than *react*.

Let's clarify this. A reaction is often done in an instant, without much thought. It's our default based upon our past. A response, however, is more thoughtful. It taps into our Spiritual Connection, our conscious mind.

Simply put: *responding is an intentional thought; reacting is without thought.*

The key to responding to the negative self-talk is to pause, notice, and acknowledge "That's not true." For example, perhaps the negative self-talk attempts to sabotage your thoughts with a message like "You can't succeed—you'll mess it up in some way." When this happens, take a moment to pause and notice the false message, then state "That's not true." Next, ask yourself, "What if I *can* succeed? What if I *don't* mess up?"

By simply stating "That's not true," we deflate the negative self-talk and move into the calm, kind voice of our inner Spiritual Connection. We get to *choose* to respond rather than react. We have a choice. We can change our thinking. We are that capable and resourceful.

This small change can shift our perception. We slowly start to change our perception of how we live our life and what we truly think of ourselves. We slowly start to shift our courage and brilliance from protection and escape to trusting our true self—our inner divinity.

When we change our perception, we change our thought. And our thought creates our reality—what we believe to be true. It allows us to challenge those negative and limiting self-beliefs. It allows us to open the door to possibility, to something different.

This is hard, hard work. A slow and deliberate process. But it works. Keep practicing.

We must be careful to never minimize or judge

the internal struggle that occurs when we face the negative self-talk. It's vital that we stay in today, in the moment, where negative self-talk cannot survive.

It's just as important to stay connected to trusted sexual assault survivors who have experienced and are experiencing this perception shift. We can learn to trust the wisdom of those who have gone before us.

Together, we can learn how to stop the negative self-talk and hear the calm, kind voice of our inner divinity. We can bring forth what is already within us: self-kindness and self-compassion.

Of all our feelings, self-compassion and self-kindness are the most difficult to bring forth—yet they are the most healing and empowering. They are our greatest weapons against the foe of negative self-talk and limiting self-beliefs.

Those deep-seated negative and limiting self-beliefs cannot compete with self-kindness and self-compassion.

When we work in tandem with our Spiritual Connection to bring forth our self-kindness and self-compassion, we can shift our perception from negative Self to empowered Self. And perception is powerful. A simple change of perception—like "That's not true"—can actually make us feel as if we're seeing our life through a pair of different eyes.

As we challenge and disprove the negative self-beliefs, we begin to trust our Spiritual Connection—our divinity. When we trust, we feel safe.

When we feel safe, we are at peace.

Hope begins in the dark, the stubborn hope that if you just show up and try to do the right thing, the dawn will come.

—ANNE LAMOTT

Gratitude Statement

"With gratitude, I am aware of the negative and limiting self-beliefs, and I work in tandem with my Spiritual Connection to respond, 'That's not true.' I am grateful for the choice."

New Practice

Begin to notice and acknowledge the negative self-talk and identify the accompanying negative and limiting self-belief. Ask yourself, "What if I'm *not* [my negative self-belief]?" Notice and practice often.

Step 4

We examine our personal relationships and identify how the sexual assault has affected our relationship with our Self and with others.

As we've discovered on our journey through steps 1 through 3, the sexual assault has rippled through our entire life, leaving us with a residue of shame, self-blame, and never-safe feelings. We've built our protective and escapist lifestyle around this residue.

Until now.

Our ability to shake off the residue comes from the awareness discovered in steps 1 through 3:

- Awareness that we have the strength and resilience to climb out of the basement and acknowledge our sexual assault

- Awareness that no matter how dark it feels, there's always a safe light under the door—waiting for us

- Awareness that we have an inherent Spiritual Connection—a connection to something greater—within us that is the source of our courage, strength, and resilience

- Awareness that we have the ability to recognize and free ourselves from the conditioned limiting and negative self-beliefs that hold us back from who we truly are

- Awareness that we have the resourcefulness to recognize and quiet the accompanying negative self-talk and make loud the Spiritual Connection within

- Awareness that when we operate from our Spiritual Connection, our created protective lifestyle and escapist behavior are no longer necessary for our survival

- Awareness that when we stay in today, in the here and now, healing happens

Now, in step 4, we get to examine and understand how the sexual assault and the accompanying residue affect our relationship with our Self and with others.

This step provides a window to view how we show up for ourselves and for others.

As sexual assault survivors, especially those of us still struggling within the residue of shame, self-blame, and never-safe feelings, we *need* our personal relationships to provide safety—physical and emotional. This includes safety from feeling shamed or judged.

But this is difficult for many of us. We spend so much time shaming and judging ourselves that we simply assume everyone else is shaming and judging us as well. This wreaks havoc on our relationships.

The bottom line is, we treat others as well as we treat ourselves. We create the relationships we think we deserve.

If we're living a protective lifestyle from a place of shame, self-blame, and never-safe, this directly affects our relationships. How can it not?

And if we're constantly battling and attempting to escape from our limiting self-beliefs and the accompanying negative self-talk, this, too, affects our relationships. Again, how can it not?

In order for us to heal and recover from the violence done to us—in order to regain our genuine true Self—it is essential that we understand how the sexual assault residue keeps us from having fulfilling relationships and possibly even keeps us in unfulfilling relationships. It is essential that we examine each of our relationships and ask ourselves a simple question: *Does this relationship honor my healing?*

At first read, this may seem like a starkly selfish statement—very contrary to many societal and religious messages that uphold "good works" and "service to others" as the utmost goal. From that standpoint, thinking of ourselves first is *wrong. Bad.* Those messages lead us to believe that we should live our life for others first. That we should always, at any cost, put others before ourselves.

However, we cannot hope to be joyous and free if we're living our life for others or by a set of rules that jump over or deny our own healing process. We cannot truly be "right" with anyone else until we are "right" with ourselves. We cannot experience true compassion and love for others until we experience compassion and true love for ourselves.

So, we examine our relationship with our Self and with others. We do this *not* to blame ourselves but rather to deepen our understanding and compassion for those parts of ourselves we want to change.

We don't change what we are,
we change what we think we are.

—Eric Butterworth

Opportunities of Examined Relationships

This step provides us many opportunities to learn about our relationships with our Self and with others. Listed below are what we consider the four key opportunities.

First, this step provides us the opportunity to examine how we show up in each relationship and how we allow others to show up.

Do we show up with a guarded and mistrusting attitude? Do we show up helpless, with no personal agency? Do we allow others to treat us with disrespect or as less than? Do we allow others to take more and give less? Do we trust our instincts and intuition, or do we follow others? Do we show up as having all the answers, with no vulnerability?

Second, this step provides us the opportunity to better understand our expectations of others.

Do we expect our relationships to fill our internal emptiness—the void within? Do we expect our relationships to save us—make us whole? Do we expect to always get our way? Do we expect perfection from ourselves and others? Do we expect honesty and truth from ourselves and others? Are we continually expecting the other shoe to drop and the relationship to fail?

Third, this step provides us the opportunity to see how our protective barriers and escapist lifestyle show up in our relationships and therefore keep us out of balance with ourselves and others.

Are our protections getting in the way of balanced, joyous relationships with others? How does our feeling of never-safe impact our physical, emotional, and financial relationships? Are we able to be vulnerable with others, or is the mere idea of letting someone "in" terrifying? Is our lack of trust in others so great that we must control every aspect of the relationship to avoid being hurt? Do we keep secrets to protect ourselves? Do we engage in uncomfortable behaviors and situations just to make others happy? Are we able to experience self-love and self-compassion as well as love and compassion for others? Do we recognize the same protective patterns across several relationships?

And fourth, this step provides us the opportunity to better understand the power of acceptance.

But before we consider the reflection questions for this fourth opportunity, let us clarify what acceptance is—and isn't.

Acceptance occurs when we reach the internal realization that the person, place, or situation before us is what it is and that we cannot change it, no matter how hard we try. It does not necessarily mean we agree with the person, place, or situation in question. It does not mean we have "settled" for less than.

An easy example of acceptance is the weather,

specifically the rain. We cannot stop the rain—no matter how hard we try, no matter how angry we become, no matter how intelligent we are, no matter how much money we have. We *accept* that it's raining. We may not be happy about it, but we know there's nothing we can do about the rain.

Now, while we can't stop the rain, we *can* change our response to it. We do not have to get wet. We can choose to use an umbrella. We can choose to go inside. We can even choose to reschedule our outdoor plans for some sunny day. We do not have to accept that the rain has ruined our day.

This explanation of acceptance applies to our sexual assault as well. It happened—we were sexually assaulted. We cannot make it un-happen. We may deny, minimize, rage, cry, but sooner or later, we accept it. It happened.

However, we do not have to accept the falsehoods that our life is ruined, that people are always out to hurt us, that nothing or no one is safe, that the assault and the accompanying residue will forever be our sad companions. These things we do not have to accept.

So, with this understanding of acceptance in mind, let's ask ourselves these questions: Are we minimizing or denying the impact of the sexual assault with ourselves and others? Are we holding the sexual assault as a shameful secret? Do we believe somewhere in the recesses of our mind that the sexual assault has ruined our chances of having a loving relationship? Are we so comfortable with our shame, self-blame, and never-safe feelings that our relationships are built around this residue?

These are a few of the opportunities we receive when we examine our relationships. And if we step into these opportunities, they will ultimately lead us to a powerful gift.

The gift of choice.

We often miss opportunity because it's dressed in overalls and looks like work.

—Anonymous

The Gift of Choice

There's power and relief in understanding what we can change and what we cannot. That power is choice.

As sexual assault survivors, many of us feel that the power of choice has been taken from us. Or that in order to be safe, we must reduce our choices to either right or wrong, good or bad, black or white. There's no room for in-between. No room for gray.

And whenever there's no room for in-between or gray choices, we put ourselves in a "safe" protective space—the basement.

But with the new level of awareness we've gleaned from steps 1 through 3, we've moved out of the basement. We now have an understanding of personal choice. We know that we *get* to decide.

It's empowering. It's compassionate. It's honest. It's truth.

So, then, how do we use our new understanding of choice in our relationships? We start by understanding that relationships are "gray" and "in-between."

For many of us, this can be an uncomfortable concept—a new place. But the gift of choice lives in this place of gray, in-between.

Next, we examine our relationship with our Self and others. Through this examination, we often discover common threads or repeating patterns in our relationships. We also discover the choices we can make within ourselves to create better relationships. For instance, perhaps we choose to learn how to pause and respond rather than angrily react. Perhaps we choose to cease "saving" others or expecting others to "save" us.

And if we're honest with ourselves, it doesn't take long to spot the relationships that need to go. Sometimes we have to choose to say goodbye to certain relationships that hold us back by feeding our negative self-beliefs and keeping our escapism active. These types of relationships do not serve our healing.

Once we begin examining our relationships and exercising our power of choice, we will notice a more powerful Spiritual Connection. We will begin to trust ourselves and our brilliant capacity to make relationship choices that serve our healing.

May your choices reflect your hopes, not your fears.
—NELSON MANDELA

Preparing to Examine Our Relationships

At this point, we may be thinking, *Just how are we supposed to "examine" our relationships? What does that even mean? How does that even work?*

This step has the potential to become an overwhelming undertaking. And when something overwhelms us, we often find an excuse not to do it.

For this reason, let's keep this step simple. The simplicity is in the questions we ask ourselves on pages 66–68. However, remember: just because something is simple doesn't mean it's easy. So, first, let's consider a few helpful tips and guidelines:

- We need to be intentional about tapping into our Spiritual Connection for courage and guidance.

- Many of us find it useful to write out our answers to each question. This helps make the process "real."
- Keep in mind there is no right or wrong way to answer these questions. All we do is tell ourselves the truth with rigorous honesty—that is, tell the truth about ourselves, and tell the truth about the people in our lives. There is power and freedom in the truth.
- To be clear, *this is not an exercise in finding out what's wrong with us or the other person*. Rather, it's our opportunity to see how we show up for ourselves, how we show up for others, and how we allow others to show up for us. It's our opportunity to empower ourselves in each relationship with understanding and compassion.
- This is not a "do it once and we're done" step. Healing is not linear. It ebbs and flows. We are always healing. For this reason, we can use this step over and over again at different times throughout our life.
- It may help to first make a list of our personal relationships. These are the individuals we interact with on a regular basis,

whether at home, at work, or socially. This list especially includes our challenging relationships. It doesn't matter how many people are on the list.

- When the list is complete, we place our own name at the top. We examine our relationship with our Self first. How we treat ourselves is a good indication of how we treat others and how we allow others to treat us.

- Remember: *doing* this step is more important than doing it "right." It's about taking action.

Taking Action: We Examine Our Relationships

Ask and answer the following questions about your relationship with your **Self**:

- In what ways do I treat myself with goodness and kindness?

- What scares me about myself?

- What do I give myself?

- What am I avoiding about myself?

- What's missing from my relationship with myself?
- How can I give myself what's missing?
- What do I need to forgive* myself for?
- What do I expect of myself?
- What do I need to accept about myself?
- What do I choose for myself?
- Where is my power?

Ask and answer the following questions for each relationship with **others**:

- What goodness do I bring to this relationship?
- What scares me about this relationship?
- What do I receive from this relationship?
- What am I avoiding in this relationship?
- What's missing from this relationship?
- How can I give myself what's missing?
- What needs to be forgiven* of myself and the other person in this relationship?

- What are my expectations of myself and the other person in this relationship?
- What do I need to accept about myself and the other person in this relationship?
- What do I choose for myself in this relationship?
- Where is my power in this relationship?

**A Word about Forgiveness*

Whenever we speak of forgiveness in this step, the intent is to focus only on the what, *not the* how. *That is, these reflection questions ask us to merely identify what needs to be forgiven. We are not so presumptive as to tell a person how to forgive.*

Forgiveness is a very personal process between an individual and their Spiritual Connection. It has no imposed timeline and cannot be rushed or dictated by others. Many of us find that as we heal with compassion and love, forgiveness begins to evolve.

Respect the evolution.

It does not matter how slowly you go
as long as you do not stop.
—CONFUCIUS

We Share Our Findings

Once we complete the examination, many of us find it extremely useful to review our findings with another trusted sexual assault survivor.

Some of us, however, may balk at this suggestion. *Our findings are private. Why do we need to share them?*

Well, we don't *need* to. This is merely a suggestion. But there are many benefits to consider.

When we share our relationship findings with a trusted survivor, we get the opportunity to hear another survivor say, "I do the same thing!" or, "I understand what you're talking about—I feel that way too," or, "I agree—we can't change others, only ourselves." We receive validation. We receive understanding. We feel seen and heard without judgment.

When we include another survivor in our process, we also experience a sense of belonging. We find out we are not alone in our pain and oversights in relationships. In particular, we relieve ourselves of the isolation that comes from being alone with our shame. Shame dies when we talk about it.

Involving another survivor also gives us the much-needed support and camaraderie to find our power within each relationship. Together, we can explore options to help bring about change—whether it be learning new ways to show up or learning ways to say goodbye.

Most importantly, each time we share our relationship stories with another trusted survivor, we open the door further to our light within—our Divine Spirit. We create an internal paradigm shift that creates a fundamental change in our approach to and our underlying assumptions for each relationship. We trust our inner Self.

And when we trust, we feel safe.

When you know you're worth something more,
you don't accept something less.

—ANNY DONEWALD AND JOSHUA ROBISON

Gratitude Statement

"With gratitude, I engage in relationships that serve my healing and allow me to thrive and flourish with compassion."

New Practice

Intentionally choose relationships that honor your resilience, healing, and truth. If you are uncertain, examine the relationship.

Step 5

With the chains of shame, self-blame, and never-safe removed and our sense of safety restored, we continue to strengthen our Spiritual Connection and share our story of healing, hope, and empowerment with other sexual assault survivors.

Shame, self-blame, and never-safe emotions are heavy, heavy chains that keep us tethered to the sexual assault—to our past. As long as we wear these chains, we carry a burden that does not belong to us. By practicing the steps in this healing process and incorporating them into our lifestyle, we can remove the chains one link at a time.

Does that mean we will never feel shame or self-blame again? That all the negative self-talk will be gone? That we will always feel safe?

Some days, we'll be without shame and self-blame. Some days, we'll shut down the negative self-talk. Some days, we'll feel completely safe. And some days, we won't.

Every day is different. Healing from sexual assault is a process without an end date. There are no absolutes; there is awareness, acknowledgement, and choice. Healing is not linear. It ebbs and it flows.

However, each time we acknowledge the source of our shame, we remove a link.

Each time we shift blame from ourselves to the perpetrator, we remove a link.

Each time we replace the negative self-talk with compassion and love, we remove a link.

Each time we consciously assess a person, place, or situation and deem it safe, we remove a link.

Each time we tap into our divinity within—our Spiritual Connection—for guidance, strength, and empowerment, we remove a link.

Each time we pause and acknowledge what's going on right now, in the present, we remove a link.

Each time we intentionally respond rather than react in our same old familiar ways, we remove a link.

Each time we reach out for help from a trusted sexual assault survivor, we remove a link.

And every time we remove a link, we trust ourselves more. When we trust ourselves, we remember who we truly are—our true Self.

When we live our life as who we truly are, we no longer need to keep life in the basement as an option.

> *So oftentimes it happens that we live our lives in chains and we never even know we have the key.*
>
> —"ALREADY GONE," PERFORMED BY THE EAGLES AND WRITTEN BY JACK TEMPCHIN AND ROBB STRANDLUND

Strengthen Our Spiritual Connection

When we continue strengthening our Spiritual Connection, we receive the necessary help, healing, and guidance to continue removing the chains that hold us back. We continue to operate from our power within. We continue to wake up the strong, capable, resourceful person we actually are.

We release our inner giant.

We begin to understand that a fulfilled life is lived from the inside out. We begin to notice that we have stopped *reacting* and are now *responding* to each situation in a way that serves us. We realize we actually *can* recognize when we're agitated, anxious, afraid, angry, or sad. We learn we have the ability to extend the pause between feeling these emotions in the moment and forming a response. By extending the pause, we no longer react out of our emotions; we respond with intention. We get to choose.

That's empowerment. That's agency.

This may seem like a daunting undertaking. For many of us, it's totally foreign. But it's certainly not impossible, and it's accessible to everyone. Just ask a trusted sexual assault survivor who has crossed over from foreign to familiar.

We have a choice about how we respond. We can practice this foreign thing until it becomes a familiar thing.

That's change.

Things do not change; we change.

—HENRY DAVID THOREAU

Deliberate Daily Practice

If we're still burdened by the lingering chains of shame, self-blame, and never-safe, it's easy to understand how our protective, survival lifestyle has become one reaction after another after another after another.

Our protective reactions are like driving our vehicle on the same snowy road over and over again. We leave just one set of tire tracks. Those tracks become so deep and packed down that it's difficult to create new tracks. It feels easier to stay in the same old familiar tracks.

Just as it feels easier to stay in our protective lifestyle. It's familiar. We know how to operate in the deep, packed-down tracks. The ruts.

If we're truly honest with ourselves, we really do want to create new tracks. But how?

By creating a deliberate daily practice that connects us to our great inner strength. Only then can we consciously create the new tracks that allow us to respond rather than react.

In the beginning, this deliberate daily practice may be as simple as pausing several times throughout the day to identify whenever we feel our chest race, our jaw clench, our neck ache, our stomach churn, or any of the many ways our bodies talk to us and signify some sort of internal distress.

At that point, we breathe. We listen. We pay attention. We notice and acknowledge what's going on *right now*. By focusing on our breathing, we slow down, we become present, and we have conscious contact with our power within. We respond intentionally rather than react emotionally.

Each time we do this, we move an inch out of the old tracks and begin to create new tracks. We remove a chain link.

Some of us are so disconnected from our bodies that we cannot feel a racing chest or a clenched jaw. That's OK. We've all been there. Especially in the beginning.

In this case, we can pick three or four times each day to pause—to stop whatever we're doing—and take three intentional deep breaths. Believe it or not, this deliberate practice is a direct connection to our body, which is a direct connection to our divinity. It's a simple way to learn to slow down and listen to our body. It's all about the connection—to the body and divinity within.

As we move forward in our healing, many of us choose to practice a more intentional conscious contact with our power within, such as meditation. One of the many purposes of meditation is to bring us into the now—the present moment.

Remember: shame, self-blame, and never-safe cannot survive in the present.

Meditation provides us a daily opportunity to *be* in the present, the moment, the right now. It can serve as our daily awareness of our internal strength, our capacity to heal, and our resilience.

There are numerous books, articles, apps, and media sites that teach meditation. Check them out and find one that appeals to your needs. Ask another trusted survivor about their meditation practice.

Meditation requires us to "shut off" our minds, which is perhaps the most frustrating part for some of us. In the beginning, it may seem nearly impossible.

We must be patient and compassionate with ourselves. This is a new practice. With all new practices, our mind will resist. Our mind will want to return to the familiar deep tracks in the snow. We are conditioned to prefer the familiar even if the familiar keeps us stuck. But this is our opportunity to step out of the familiar and create a practice to strengthen our Spiritual Connection.

Many of us have found it extremely useful to create a gratitude statement and repeat it throughout our meditation. Here are a few examples:

- *With gratitude, I am safe.*
- *I am grateful to love myself.*
- *With gratitude, I am compassionate toward others and myself.*
- *With gratitude, I am free of self-blame.*
- *With gratitude, I am free of shame.*

Create your own gratitude statement, and repeat it to coincide with your breathing. Start out slowly. Try three minutes each day. The benefits are subtle but immediate.

A word of caution: expect the negative self-talk chatter to rear up. Your chatter may tell you this "gratitude meditation" is pointless and silly.

When this happens, just pause, acknowledge

the negative self-talk, state "That's not true," and move on.

Be aware, too, that each gratitude statement may feel like an untruth in the beginning. We may feel that we really *aren't* grateful, we really *don't* feel safe, or we really *don't* love ourselves.

That's OK. Actually, it's expected. Again, we're doing something new and unfamiliar. We're creating new tracks, removing links of chains.

Once again, acknowledge the negative self-talk and respond with self-compassion. We must be kind to ourselves while we learn this new practice.

We are at the place of choice: we can follow the negative self-talk that only serves to sabotage our healing, or we can remove our chains and create freedom through our deliberate practice. We always have a choice.

If we desire to get better, we opt for the deliberate daily practice of meditation regardless of how uncomfortable it is. The discomfort of learning a new practice is temporary; the benefits and personal rewards of a strong Spiritual Connection are endless.

But first of all we shall want sunlight;
nothing much can grow in the dark.
Meditation is our step out into the sun.

—Alcoholics Anonymous World Services

Share Our Story

We now come to perhaps the most important piece of our healing journey: sharing our personal story of hope, healing, and empowerment with other sexual assault survivors. And sharing our story of hope, healing, and empowerment means we actually *believe* we have a story of hope, healing, and empowerment.

Think about that statement. In order to share a healing-empowerment story, we must believe we have one. And to believe we have a healing-empowerment story, we, at some point, must have experienced a shift from the dark basement to the light.

This is a transformation.

Hope, healing, and empowerment are within us all—have been since the day we were born. By coming out of the basement and into the light, we have awakened these great inner powers. It is now time to free them.

We free them by telling our story so others can have hope, healing, and empowerment. Sharing with other sexual assault survivors how we received these gifts is the very thing that makes life worthwhile and full of purpose.

Keep in mind that we share our story not to "save" other survivors but to bear witness that a life beyond mere surviving actually exists. We are here to stand tall, to thrive and flourish beyond our survival.

We are the story of what's possible after sexual assault. We are the hope. We are the healing. We are the empowerment. We all need to feel our strength. The world needs to see our strength. We share the gift.

Keep in mind, as well, that sharing our story doesn't mean becoming an open book with no boundaries or guide rails. Our story is *our personal story*. We get to decide when we share, what we share, and how we share. We are the sole driver of our story bus.

A special word of caution: if we only share the details of our assault, we remain in the trauma of our assault. And it keeps others in the trauma of their assaults as well. We all stay stuck in the tragedy rather than moving into the freedom of hope, healing, and empowerment. Rather, let's remember that the focus of our sharing is to create hope, healing, and empowerment for the listener and to reinforce and strengthen our own journey.

When we share our out-of-the-basement story, we share our inner strength—our Spiritual Connection. We become stronger. We increase trust in ourselves. We come to understand that delivering our story and shifting our focus to another survivor causes our own pain to lessen. We come to understand that our struggle out of the darkness is actually our greatest gift. It is the light that can guide others out of the isolation of sexual assault.

We can all perhaps remember what it was like to hear the story of another survivor for the first time. It seemed like the beginning of the end of our isolation. There was a person, sharing their story—*our* story. *Finally, someone who gets it!* we exclaimed to ourselves.

While the details of our individual stories are unique, the residual effects of shame, self-blame, and never-safe are the same. We all carry those chains. It's part of our shared experience.

We share these same chains regardless of the "degrees" and "levels" in which our stories differ. That is, we do not feel "more" or "less" shame, self-blame, or never-safe emotions than other survivors.

These residual emotions do not discriminate; neither should we. We cannot afford to separate ourselves from one another based upon perceived degrees or levels of seriousness of sexual assault. We are *not* separate. We are connected by a shared experience as well as by our desire to heal. Regardless of the details.

Sharing our story allows us to feel compassion for ourselves and to show compassion to others. When we show compassion, caring, and love to other survivors, we experience a deep joy that we can receive in no other way. It is a gift.

By sharing our story of hope, healing, and empowerment, we show others that there is life after sexual assault—a thriving life. Thriving is not measured by money, possessions, or career but by inner strength, resilience, and self-love.

We show others that personal agency is possible. We can be in charge of our life. We have a say in what happens to us. We have the ability to shape our circumstances to our best interests.

Most importantly, though, our brilliant stories of resilience to overcome the past offer an invitation to heal. We show other survivors what's possible. We transcend together, out of the basement and beyond surviving.

That's a powerful message indeed.

Tell the story of the mountain you climbed.
Your words could become a page in
someone else's survival guide.

—MORGAN HARPER NICHOLS

Gratitude Statement

"With gratitude, I am no longer chained to the past. I am safe. With gratitude, I share my story of healing, hope, and empowerment."

New Practice

Create a deliberate practice of daily connection to your inner divinity. Express to the Universe, the Divine Spirit, God—whatever is your Something Greater—a willingness to share your healing story, then wait for the opportunity to be presented.

PART II

DO:
Creating Community

Guidelines for Creating Community

A single twig breaks, but the bundle of twigs is strong.

—TECUMSEH

We cannot experience the full transformation of healing, hope, and empowerment alone. It is experienced in community with other sexual assault survivors. As survivors, we understand the experience of a sexual assault like no one else can. This common understanding—this shared experience—provides a sense of safety and belonging that many of us need to keep healing.

Sharing our healing stories, supporting one another, strengthening one another, and telling our truth to one another inspires each of us to continue the upward spiral—our ascent out of the basement. When we gather in groups of like-minded, understanding survivors, we can work together to bring our best selves into the present and out of our past.

Together, we can transcend beyond surviving. Together, we can thrive.

The key is that this must be a *safe* community. Safety and trust are hard for many of us. We need a community where we know we can express our pain and continue our healing without judgment or further trauma.

It can be challenging to find this type of community. We're so conditioned to remain silent and keep the "secret" that many of us struggle to find a safe community that understands us and that we can belong to.

An easy option is to create your own support community. Since many of us already know at least two or three other sexual assault survivors, creating a support community may not be difficult.

Here, then, are some recommended guidelines for creating an accessible, responsive, safe community of sexual assault survivors who are ready to take their healing to the next phase—beyond surviving.

Name the Community

Who are we? Choose a name for the community. The name helps identify this as a community for survivors of sexual assault. The name can also help describe the community's purpose (see below). For example: Beyond Surviving.

Define the Community's Purpose

What is our purpose? Defining the community's purpose puts safety perimeters—boundaries—around the community. Defining our purpose communicates the focus and vision for the community. We feel safe when we know what to expect. Here's an example of a purpose statement:

> *Beyond Surviving is a community for sexual assault survivors. It is a safe and confidential community of individuals who gather to share their healing, hope, and empowerment after sexual assault and to help other sexual assault survivors heal, become hopeful, and empower themselves on a daily basis. Our primary purpose is to support one another to achieve joy and freedom by focusing on this healing, hope, and empowerment. We believe joy and freedom are possible for everyone after a sexual assault—any sexual assault.*

Create a Community Value Statement

What do we value as a community? Set forth the community values so each member knows what to expect. Defining our values communicates our focus and vision. It also puts safety perimeters—boundaries—around the community. In this way, defining our values is an extension of defining our purpose.

Here's an example of a value statement as a bulleted list:

- *We value every sexual assault survivor's story of healing, hope, and empowerment. Every story is filled with strength, resilience, and truth.*

- *We value and respect the healing process of each sexual assault survivor. We acknowledge that healing is not a linear process; it ebbs and it flows. There is no right or wrong, good or bad, quick or slow way to heal. Each individual determines their own healing process. We keep moving forward together.*

- *We value and honor the safety of each sexual assault survivor within this community. We commit to keeping this a safe space, where the focus is on healing, hope, and empowerment rather than on the traumatic details of the assault.*

- *We value the confidentiality of each member of this community. The names of individual community members will not be shared outside of the community.*

- *We value providing each member with the opportunity to be seen and heard within the community. This is a safe place for members to share their stories and struggles with healing, hope, and empowerment. This safety depends upon keeping the community free from cross talk or feedback during gatherings. Our healing depends upon our sense of safety to share without judgment or comment from others.*

- *We value community decision-making and equality. There are no leaders, facilitators, or hierarchies. Rather, we follow a community-determined meeting format, and we rotate among peer volunteers to guide the group through the format.*

- *We value freedom and choice. There are no requirements for attendance other than being a survivor of sexual assault—any sexual assault.*

- *We value and focus on healing, hope, and empowerment for all sexual assault survivors, and we review and discuss literature with the same focus. Literature selection is a community decision.*

- *We value and respect each individual's time. The community will decide the length of each meeting.*

- *We value the transformation of community healing and the gratitude that accompanies such a transformation.*

Determine the Location

Where do we meet? As a community, agree upon a safe, neutral location for meeting. The selected location will allow the community to adhere to the agreed-upon purpose and values, especially safety and respect.

Create a Community Meeting Format

What do we do together? As a community, determine what meeting format to follow. This will allow the community to stay true to the agreed-upon purpose and values, and it will also provide clear expectations for each gathering. A meeting format is especially important for groups who value equality and wish to operate without a leader or facilitator.

In discussing the meeting format, the community should determine the meetings' frequency and length (such as once a month for an hour), schedule (see example below), and guidance structure (such as having community members volunteer to be part of a rotation to guide the group through the schedule).

Here's a sample schedule, based on an hour-long meeting with a rotating volunteer guide, a literature reading, and a sharing time:

- *Welcome community members, and extend special welcome to individuals attending for the first time.*
- *Read the Purpose Statement.*
- *Read the Value Statement.*
- *Briefly explain how the meeting works.*
- *Begin introductions.*
- *Read the selected literature.*
- *Begin sharing, with each member choosing to share or pass.*
- *Close the gathering after the agreed-upon length of time has passed.*

Never doubt that a small group of thoughtful, committed citizens can change the world; indeed, it's the only thing that ever has.

—MARGARET MEAD

PART III

SHARE:
Personal Stories

PART III—SHARE: PERSONAL STORIES

The final portion of this book contains the personal stories of seven sexual assault survivors. The stories have been personally written by each survivor—in their own words. Each story title was created by the individual writer-survivor.

The primary focus of each story is the survivor's journey of healing, hope, and empowerment. Their journey out of the basement.

As a cautionary warning, please know that each story includes a reference to sexual assault, albeit general and brief.

There is no greater agony than bearing
an untold story inside you.

—Maya Angelou

The Cycle Stops Now

I was raised by two very fractured and damaged parents. They were raised, in turn, by fractured and damaged parents. And so on and so on. We are what we learn—until we learn something new.

Sadly, my parents never learned anything new. They continued the cycle of sexual abuse and violence against my siblings and me.

I have learned something new. The cycle of sexual abuse stops with me. Now.

During my childhood and teenage years, I lived in a sort of psychosphere of dysfunction. I grew up in a family and within a community that practiced various dark cult rituals and participated in sex trafficking. I was forced to participate in both. Sexual assaults by my father and other male extended family members occurred with some regularity.

I learned at a very young age that I was on my own. Safety did not exist.

As a child, I had an enormous capacity to adapt

to the most horrific circumstances, though I wasn't aware that that's what I was doing. I was just trying to survive.

For me, the best explanation of this "adapting" capacity is described by Maya Angelou in *I Know Why the Caged Bird Sings*. She says, "Children's talent to endure stems from their ignorance of alternatives." So true.

I was ignorant of anything different—ignorant of alternatives. So, I got up every morning and started another day. No other option. No one ever talked about or even acknowledged the abuse, the violence, the rituals, or the trafficking. It was simply never discussed.

My siblings and I had been conditioned to keep silent by numerous and varied threats of violence. So, that's what I did. I kept silent. I didn't want to be hurt, and I didn't want to see one of my siblings get hurt. I was not allowed to resist. I was conditioned to expect violent treatment from adults.

I remember as a child having an achy, empty feeling around my heart and a constant upset stomach. I very often had a cold sore on my bottom lip, and I suffered from numerous urinary tract infections. I now know this was my body's response to anxiety.

When I was a small child, I would leave my body during the abuse. I'd see myself running down a hallway and hiding around the corner. I was safe there. No one could see me.

As a teenager, I would leave my body and go up to the ceiling when I was being abused. I would look down on what was happening as if it were happening to someone else.

I now know that's the brilliant coping skill of dissociation. Dissociating and disconnecting became my greatest and, eventually, most complicated coping mechanisms.

When I was about eight or nine, my sister told me a story about a little boy who died of a broken heart. According to the story, the little boy's parents didn't love him, and he had no friends. So, one day while walking to school, he lay down in a snowbank and died. He died all alone of a broken heart.

I have no idea if there's any truth to this story, but at the time, I truly understood what that little boy was feeling. That's how I felt—achy and empty around my heart. I was very afraid I would die of a broken heart, just like that little boy. I didn't want to die.

It was around this time that I completely disconnected from my body and from the reality of my life. I started to pretend. I pretended my heart didn't ache. I pretended my stomach didn't hurt. I pretended the sexual abuse and violence didn't bother me, didn't affect me. I pretended my family and home life were wonderful.

I pretended everything was great.

I created and lived within a reality that did not exist. I shut down all emotion. I refused to acknowledge what was happening, because to do so would kill me, I thought.

This was my coping mechanism for many, many years. I repressed all my assault memories—stuffed them into a secret closet and triple-locked the door with multiple chains.

To this day, I am astounded by my capacity to deny what was actually happening around me. I had no idea how hard I was working to protect myself. My instinct to survive knew few bounds.

But the one thing I couldn't pretend was "great" was me. Within me was an underlying knowledge and deep belief that I wasn't any good. That something was wrong with me inside. I wasn't exactly sure what, but I knew that I was definitely unlovable and that I deserved to be hurt.

From a child's logic, this made sense. It *had* to be my fault. Why else was I being abused and hurt? This deep, deep belief was branded into my psyche with every sexually violent act perpetrated against me: I was no good, unlovable.

As I got older, this inner hollowness grew into a chasm. At the age of twelve, I was introduced to alcohol and drugs. It was amazing—in the beginning. *Finally*, I thought, *the solution to all my problems.* I could drink alcohol and smoke weed to oblivion and escape my life.

I spent the next five years either drunk or high or planning the next time I could be drunk or high. The more I drank and got high, the less I cared about myself or anyone else. I was achingly lonely and filled with tremendous self-hate. The alcohol and the drugs provided an escape from all that.

Just before my eighteenth birthday, I was arrested for driving drunk, open bottle, and possession of an illegal substance. I was sent to a drug and alcohol rehabilitation center for thirty days.

This truly was the best thing that had ever happened to me in my short seventeen years of life. It got me away from my family and the dysfunctional community. I was in an environment that, while not completely ideal, was better than home.

I threw myself into the recovery program during and after my stay in rehab. I immersed myself in the whole recovery process. It seemed to fill the void left by alcohol and drugs—and the deeper void left by all the abuse. When I left for college six months later, it felt like I had finally found something I was good at, something I could do right.

But I still couldn't shake the pull of my parents or that dysfunctional community. The dark cult rituals and sex trafficking were still active in the community and within my family. I was conditioned to come home and participate. It was an unspoken expectation.

My self-hate, especially my bodily hate, grew worse. My pretending to live in a made-up reality intensified.

But all the while, I continued to develop a life within the alcohol-drug recovery community. I had a support system and a community in which I belonged. I had people around me who genuinely cared about me. I'd never experienced that before. I began to trust a few of them. I also began to develop and believe in a Spiritual Connection, a link to something greater, a divine source within me.

I slowly, slowly started to feel empowered. I started to feel like there was actually something different—something better—for me than what I was living.

I started to make some changes. I left a very sick and abusive relationship with a boyfriend I'd had since high school. I decided *not to go home* during the first summer after college. Instead, I decided to be on my own, to get a job and support myself. I started a small business of cleaning houses. This was the first time I dared to challenge and resist the conditioning.

I was sober. I was out of that violent relationship. And I was away from my family. It felt good.

Until it was all ripped away.

I was sexually assaulted by one of my clients while I was cleaning his apartment. I was in shock, in disbelief. *How could this happen? What was I thinking, cleaning houses for strangers? I'm an idiot.*

I never told anyone I'd been raped. I never called the police. I stuffed this assault and the debilitating shame into the secret closet and slammed the door shut. I felt lost, forsaken, completely alone. This nearly pushed me over the edge of sanity.

So, I did what was familiar. I went back to my family. I rekindled the abusive relationship with my boyfriend. I fell deeply into my pretend, created reality. I dissociated, disconnected.

I did not drink or use drugs, though. I don't know why, other than it was one of those times in my life where God's grace was doing for me what I could not do for myself.

I returned to college in the fall and resumed my immersion into the recovery community. They were good people. Safe people. They genuinely cared about me without asking for anything in return.

However, I continued to keep my secrets locked away. I continued to live within my created reality. I was unsure of what was truly real, but I didn't care.

I lived disconnected from my emotions and reality for several more years. But at the same time . . . I was slowly making changes in my life.

My Spiritual Connection was getting stronger. I learned about "pick your pain" and made some painful choices that actually benefited me.

I especially began to notice that every time I went home, I wanted to get drunk or high. That was a dangerous way to feel. It scared me.

So, slowly, slowly, I began to separate myself from my family and their community. This took years.

Looking back on it now, I believe I needed those years to get ready—ready to open that locked door. I established a support system. I stockpiled courage. I became mentally healthy so I would be ready to address the years of sexual abuse and violence.

When I was twenty-six, I experienced the first of many flashback memories. It manifested as a picture in my mind. I saw what had happened to me.

It's difficult to effectively explain what occurs when a trauma memory surfaces. It's like a dream, but it's not. I thought I was making it up—but at the same time I knew, deep within, that it was the truth.

More memories came to me, one at a time. All in that fuzzy, dreamlike state. For me, it was a slow unwinding process—an emptying of the closet a little bit at a time.

And with every memory that surfaced, a part of my pretend reality died. It felt like my life was dying. I guess, in a way, it was.

When I told my parents about a few of the first memories that surfaced, they became extremely angry. They accused me of lying and trying to hurt them. Three of my four siblings turned against me, accusing me of intentionally hurting our parents with my lies.

The family reaction was like an explosion. I had dared to speak the unspeakable, and now I was being ostracized and punished. The response completely shattered what was left of my created reality. I felt like I had been stripped of everything I knew and believed in. The emotional and physical pain was excruciating.

But it did not take me over.

There was an inner knowing, an inner guidance, an inner power that kept me moving. I got up every morning and started a new day, like when I was a child. Divine intervention kept me moving forward. I had a support system in place, a net to catch me every time I fell.

I never doubted my memories. I consider myself fortunate in that regard.

Over the years, I've known many survivors who struggle to believe their assault memories, who struggle to believe the truth of their own recollection. I can certainly see how a person can get stuck in doubt. Doubting ourselves is just one more way to blame and harm ourselves. That's familiar.

Perhaps I never doubted my memories because one of my sisters had many of the same memories. It was a corroboration, a validation of what I knew to be the truth. Her courage and strength inspired my own courage and strength.

My healing process ebbed and flowed. I spent many years unable to stay alone in my own home. Being alone at night never felt safe. I was terrified of being hurt. I was always on high alert for "intruders." I spent many years waking up several times a night to check that all the doors were locked. Some nights I'd check the doors three or four times.

I was rageful for a long time, then I wasn't. I tried to control all my relationships to protect myself from inevitable betrayal.

For the longest time, I was constantly triggered by some reminder of my past: a smell, a sound, a voice tone, a look, a physical movement, the outside temperature. These triggers caused me high agitation and irritation, plus anger.

Trauma is a peculiar animal. It stayed caged in my body and mind until I released it. I released it by talking about the years of abuse with trauma-informed therapists and other survivors. By facing the truth—my true reality.

What I've experienced throughout the past thirty-five years of this healing journey is that the Universe, the god of my understanding, provides a balance. Just when the depression, the grief, and the pain seemed too much to bear, something positive would happen. A phone call from another survivor. A recommendation for a powerful book. A song with healing lyrics. A successful outcome at work.

Recognizing the balance helped me trust my Spiritual Connection. Helped me believe I hadn't been forsaken or abandoned. Helped me understand that sometimes gratitude shows up in the dark.

Today, I can stay alone in my house. I feel safe.

Today, I recognize and feel the anxiety of a trauma trigger and know how to manage it.

Today, my relationships heal rather than harm.

Today, I trust myself and my god within.

Today, I share my story.

The cycle stops now.

Calling It What It Is

I was sexually assaulted by my older cousin when I was a young girl. I don't remember how old I was. I'm guessing it happened between the ages of six and nine.

I actually don't remember many details of it at all. I remember my cousin suddenly—without saying anything—putting his hand down my pants and touching me between my legs. I remember him putting my hand down his pants. The first time this happened we were playing in a fort with tunnels in the basement and other children were present—but off in a different tunnel. The adults were upstairs visiting.

My cousin lived in a different state, so I didn't see him very often. But I dreaded when he came to visit. I hoped that somehow what had happened on a past visit would be forgotten and never attempted again. But eventually, at some point during each visit, it would happen. I can say for sure that this happened over the course of three separate visits. It could have been more.

I know that the last time he sexually assaulted me, something more was attempted—but I'm not sure exactly what. I didn't know what intercourse was at the time, so I had no framework for understanding it. Once I did learn about intercourse, I wondered whether that was what my cousin had tried to do.

I've always been amazed that I actually don't know what happened. I have almost no memory of that night. It's incredible how my mind blocks it all out and only allows certain small details—like the bed and the side of the room it was on and the words he used to coerce me, listing all the nice things he had done for me that day and insisting that I owed him something in return.

Although I didn't know anything about sex, I knew enough to feel ashamed and to feel that I had done something wrong. I was sworn to secrecy by my cousin and told I'd get in big trouble if I said anything; after all, I was guilty of participating in the shameful act and, as he pointed out, was therefore equally to blame. As a child, I didn't see the flaw in his logic, so it made a lot a sense to keep the secret and stay out of trouble.

I remember the day my older brother tried to get me in trouble by saying something to our mom about my cousin and I touching each other's private parts. I was horrified that he knew! How did he know? I denied it vehemently and cried hard about the accusation, feeling really scared that my mom would surely see through all this and discover the truth. She didn't.

When I got older, I remember reflecting back on this incident and being so disappointed that my mom didn't recognize that I was protesting too much. It seemed so obvious—like a kid holding something behind her back while denying that she was hiding anything.

I'm sure every bone of my mom's body wanted to believe that my cousin, a guy who was so charming and held in such high esteem by everyone in the family, would never do such a thing as sexually assault a young girl like me. We tend to see what we want to see, and not see what we don't want to see.

As I grew into a young adult and learned about sexual abuse, it occurred to me that my cousin likely sexually assaulted other young people. I worried about my much younger cousin, Mary. Did he do the same thing to her? He saw her more often than he ever saw me.

I told my aunt, Mary's mother, about the sexual assaults. She was horrified—but added that surely nothing had happened to Mary, because Mary would have fought him off. She noted that Mary wasn't as much of a people pleaser as I was.

OK, that stung. I know my aunt didn't mean to suggest that the assault was partly my fault since I didn't fight back, but that was the not-so-subtle message I heard. People pleaser or not, my cousin's sexual assault of me was not my fault.

This brings up a really important point about what we need to do to protect young children from sexual assault. It's *not* about teaching kids the skills to prevent this. That puts the burden on the children and subtly suggests that if children fall victim to sexual assault, then it's partly their fault. **It's never their fault.**

The focus needs to be on educating and monitoring the people who do the abusing. And who are those people? They are our family members, our family friends, our neighbors, and other trusted adults as well as nice, polite, well-behaved adolescent children within our circle. Every parent needs to know that. Everyone needs to be educated about who is doing the abuse, how frequently it happens, and how individuals can deal with sexual urges in appropriate ways. It's a parent's job to keep their kid safe—not a kid's job to keep themselves safe.

My parents, aunts, and uncles failed to keep me safe. Luckily, I rarely saw my cousin. He got married at a young age, and visits between our family and his didn't happen much. When the family gathered for reunions, he was never there, much to my relief.

And so the whole series of sexual assaults got

pushed aside in my mind; it wasn't something I thought about. I didn't deny that it had happened, but I didn't see any lasting effects it had had on my life.

I did learn, however, to be on high alert for being "used" or taken advantage of—especially by guys. My three older brothers made it very clear to me that guys frequently dated girls to get sex from them, and then they'd brag about it to other guys. These girls were not respected or liked. I was determined I'd never be used.

I remember going on a first date with an older guy. After taking me to a movie, he expected me to have sex with him. I said no way. He said I owed it to him after the money he'd spent on me. I couldn't believe he was so blatant and crass, expecting that sex with me could be bought. I got out of his car immediately and never saw him again.

When Deb Halvorson asked if I'd share my story for this book, I was willing but not sure what I could add. What happened to me seemed so common and so minor, and it'd really never had much effect on my life. I didn't think I had a healing story to offer.

But then I read the first sentence of Deb's book: *We acknowledge we were sexually assaulted and that it was not our fault.*

Was I really sexually assaulted? I guess I was, but I'd never thought of it that way before. As I wrote this story, the impact of writing and saying out loud "I was sexually assaulted by my older cousin" was huge. The gravity of it hit.

I thought of my young self and had so much compassion for her. I imagined grabbing her in my arms, telling her how much I loved her, marveling at her bravery and ability to bear what happened and cope all on her own—and so young and vulnerable.

Then I said out loud and wrote down "It was not my fault." I said it and really meant it. And that was huge. Prior to saying that, I'd still felt a tiny bit responsible. It felt really good to say definitively and without shame "It was not my fault in any way."

I imagined hugging that little girl that was me. I told her my cousin was wrong in what he did. I told her it was the adults' job to protect me and prevent this from happening, and they failed. I told her I love her and am so proud of her.

Whatever the little me did to survive and make it to adulthood—well done. The grown-up me can take it from here.

What Would Olivia Do?

April 26, 2009. I spent the afternoon watching my two-year-old niece's first gymnastics event. Spending time with family made me think about my boys and how empty the house was.

I decided to stop by my storage unit to grab some photo albums that I normally resisted the urge to look at. Losing my boys had broken me in ways I still can't fully comprehend. Pictures sometimes helped. Instead of receiving comfort, however, I was sexually assaulted by an acquaintance. I knew he was a man with limited values and few morals, but I had no idea what he was capable of. I quickly found out when he beat me and threw me in the back seat of his car.

I don't remember much about the first few minutes after the assault. Pieces of memory floated in and out of consciousness for years after. Imagine trying to put together a puzzle knowing you don't have all the pieces. It was maddening.

There were a few constants, however; details as present now as the day it happened. The taste of blood. The sound of rain hitting the roof of the car. The way my cheek exploded when he hit me. The stench of old sneakers. I was attacked in the back seat of his car, and it smelled like the pair of red-and-black Jordan basketball shoes on the floor. My stomach still churns when I get a whiff of that smell.

I had no idea what to do as I drove away from the storage facility. I thought back to all the *Law & Order: SVU* episodes I had watched. Olivia Benson is my television soulmate. I loved the show because, inevitably, Olivia and gang would catch the bad guy and ensure he was punished. It helped me believe in abstract concepts like justice and hope, especially when the world around me seemed devoid of it.

So, I imagined myself at Olivia's police station. She would want to bring me to a hospital. But that was the last thing I wanted to do. The thought of anyone, even a medical professional, touching me filled my mouth with stomach acid. I was a year clean and sober at this point, desperately trying to get off the road to nowhere that I had been traveling. But now I just wanted to get high. I wanted to forget. I wanted to die. I began to spin out.

In recovery, one often hears people talk about things happening "by the grace of God." It took me a long time to understand what that meant, even longer to figure out how it applied to me. I worried that I had used up all of God's grace or at least had lost the privilege of receiving it. Somehow, however, he was still there. By the grace of God, I didn't drive to a dealer or to the liquor store. Instead, I called Rhonda, my sponsor, and asked if I could come over. I don't even remember dialing the phone, but I did. Or maybe someone did it for me.

I didn't tell Rhonda all that had happened, but she could see the bruises. She was worried I might have a concussion. After talking me into going to the emergency room, she began to ask me questions. I couldn't articulate the way I had been violated, so I told her it had been just a fight. The next day, she came to her own conclusion. Thinking I'd only been physically assaulted, she assumed I'd gotten into trouble while trying to score drugs. I didn't correct her accusation. It seemed easier to let her think the worst of me and my recovery than it was to tell her that I had been raped.

Looking back now, it is difficult to understand why I felt I'd rather be considered a drug addict than a victim. Shame is a vicious beast.

It took two days, but I finally revealed what had happened. I went to the hospital for a rape kit and to the police station to make a report. In theory, these actions should have helped me take my power back. At least that is what Olivia would have told me. In reality, however, it was just a different kind of victimization. I had to relay what had happened, over and over. Saliva, blood, hair, and urine samples. DNA and cervical swabs. Photographs. I cried at times; panic-attacked my way through others. Question after question. Repetition after repetition. My answers came out in sobs, screams, and stutters. Sometimes nothing came out at all.

The nurses and cops were nice, or at least I could tell they were trying—until the end of the rape exam. Throughout the entire ordeal, I had been dealing with one nurse, and I was beginning to feel a bit of comfort around her. But then she said something as I was getting dressed.

"I'm going to ask another nurse to finish the exam," she said.

I didn't understand.

"I have a religious objection to providing some of the preventative medications," she added.

She then explained that she was referring to the morning-after pill. I could feel my face getting hot as she talked. My chest constricted, and I had trouble breathing.

You have a religious objection to a pill that will prevent me from getting pregnant with my rapist's child? You would rather I carry his child than give me a pill that has absolutely no effect on you? How fucking sanctimonious!

I felt like bashing her head in with the tray she was holding. Instead, I just cried.

I was once asked how I thought my rape impacted me the most. I still have trouble articulating an appropriate answer, but I know I have many things in common with the victims I see on *Law & Order: SVU*. Getting raped led me to erect a barrier between me and the rest of the world. I was convinced that another attack would be imminent if I didn't remain vigilant. I didn't trust the people already in my life, and I certainly didn't allow anyone new close enough to hurt me. I rarely left the safety of my home, and I actively avoided large groups when I did. I was terrified of the dark.

The biggest impact was internal, however. I was broken, deeply shattered into so many pieces that I didn't know how to make myself whole again—or even where to start. There was a blackness inside of me that grew a bit larger each day, actively working to engulf anything that had survived the attack. It almost consumed me . . . but even at my lowest, there was a spark. A tiny part of me that wanted to live, that wanted to thrive. I hung on to that spark with every ounce of strength I had left.

Eventually, I was able to build a small fire. And then a blaze. I just couldn't let that man take more than he already had.

A few years passed, and I thought that I had moved past the attack, that I had successfully put it behind me. Instead, I had merely buried it. The memories, the feelings, the intrusive thoughts . . . they were gone. Except they weren't. Looking back now, I can see the ways the attack manifested itself. Nightmares progressively got worse. I lashed out at those close to me without knowing why. I controlled food because I felt so out of control everywhere else. My life had become a series of rules and regulations, all designed to avoid fearful situations. But after a while, and before I'd realized it, everything had become a fearful situation. I was paralyzed.

The problem was that I wasn't fighting an external enemy. I was the enemy.

One night, I accidentally hit my wife during a bad nightmare. My lack of sleep started affecting my work. The urge to drink or use was becoming unbearable. And I was pushing my wife toward leaving me. The spark to survive—the spark I had held on to since the rape—was flickering.

Seven years after I had been attacked, I finally asked for help and started therapy. It is the best thing I could have done. I had to face what had happened before I could become the best version of myself. The days of reliving what had happened were hard. I cried and cried. And then cried some more. But slowly, the blackness dissipated, and that spark inside me began to grow stronger. Throughout it all, I was able to hold on to the determination that my rapist would not beat me. That asshole wouldn't win.

Through therapy, I realized I had to talk to the woman who had been attacked, the woman I used to be. As Olivia Benson would have confirmed, it wasn't that woman's fault. On a logical level, I agreed with that sentiment. She hadn't done anything wrong. At the core of my being, however, I blamed her. Why did she stop by the storage unit? Why didn't she leave when he drove up? Why didn't she run? She should have fought back. She should have done something, anything. Instead, she allowed herself to get attacked and, in the process, once again proved how weak and incompetent she was.

Those were the messages I sent myself, over and over and over. I didn't even realize that those words were playing on a loop. But every time I heard them, I hated myself a bit more. I got to the point where there was little left inside to hold on to; I was almost completely gone.

Luckily, whatever was left was enough.

I am very fortunate to have a spouse who stood by me through the ups and downs—which was especially difficult because most days were downs. I wanted to be her partner, but that was an impossible task until I stopped despising myself. As cliché as it sounds, I needed to be able to love myself before I could build a life with her. We can go places now without worrying about panic attacks or tantrums. Our plans no longer need to end when the sun goes down. We often explore new places, something out of the question before therapy.

The biggest change is simply that I am present

in our relationship. I am not in the back seat of that car. I am not being raped. I am not stuck in the past. There are still bad days. That is okay. It took me quite a while to realize that. I am not perfect, and I don't always make the best decisions. That is okay. Sometimes the dark seems too overwhelming to tackle, so I stay home. That is okay. There are times when my skin crawls and I can feel his touch again. That is okay. Life can be messy and frustrating. That is okay.

Regardless of what happens, I get up each morning and do my best. Some days, my best is pretty good. Others, it's poor. I keep putting one foot in front of the other, however. I am alive. I made it out of the back seat of that car. Nobody can take that from me.

I wouldn't wish a sexual assault on anyone. It isn't like what you see on television, where the woman enters some kind of trance and the world goes quiet around her. It is messy and loud. The pain all blurs together at some point, which actually helps. For weeks after, I would take shower after shower after shower, scrubbing my body in a futile attempt to feel clean or at least feel less dirty and tarnished.

Recovery was slow. But somehow, I was able to make it out the other side. I don't think I'll ever be able to say that I am grateful for my attack, but I like the person I have become, and getting raped is part of my journey. Take that away, and I have a different story. I like the one I am currently writing, however, so I embrace all its chapters.

Olivia would be proud.

Finding Beauty in the Mystery, and Peace in the Uncertainty

It wasn't sexual assault. Holding me down with his body while I repeatedly shouted "Stop!" and "No!" over and over. And even after I freed myself and rolled onto the floor from the couch, there he was again, on top of me. The weight of his body not lifting as I continued to yell "No!" and "Stop!"

We were in our swimsuits. I was entirely exposed and vulnerable. He said, "Don't you want me to be your first?" He knew sex was something I had not yet engaged in.

The other details of what he did to me aren't necessary to repeat . . . But it wasn't sexual assault. He was my best guy friend. We were really drunk. He apologized for his behavior later on. He technically didn't "touch" me "down there." We had kissed earlier in the night, so maybe it was my fault for leading him on. It was simply an inappropriate altercation between two drunk friends.

These words I told myself were a sneaky and brilliant coping mechanism. A coping mechanism to cover up the betrayal I felt from one of my best friends. The embarrassment. The shame. Dear god, the shame.

What was wrong with me? Why didn't I want to have sex with him that night? Was I supposed to have done what he said? Is this how it works in the real world? Is this what real sex is like? I was only in high school, so I truly didn't know.

What was wrong with me?

I told my close girlfriends the next day. One of them said, "Wow, he basically raped you." I shook my head and said, "Nah."

And that was that. It was brushed off as something that had happened to me . . . in the same way it had happened to so many of my friends or friends of friends. These inappropriate drunk encounters (we never referred to them as sexual assaults) were just what happened when girls drank with boys. And they would get shrugged off.

A few years later, I told another friend, but it was only to sympathize with her own story, which had left her asking, *Was it sexual assault?* I had the same question about my story. But again, I shrugged it off.

A few more years later, I wrote about it in my journal, along with a few other "inappropriate encounters" that had happened to me. *But it doesn't feel like sexual assault, you know, emotionally* . . . is what I wrote in my journal. Aren't victims of sexual assault supposed to have things like PTSD? And control issues? And anxiety disorders and eating disorders and addiction problems? I didn't have any of that.

Or so I thought. The anger came seven years later, when some level of my subconscious couldn't bear the suppression of that night anymore.

One evening, I was on a walk with a new guy friend, and he tried to hold my hand. I simply moved my hand, put a smile on, and pretended like it hadn't happened. But when I got home, I realized how wildly violated I felt.

And then, just like that, I realized what had really happened that night in high school. And how, for all these years, I had put a smile on and pretended like it hadn't happened. How, instead of opening the door to the emotions and the truth about that night, I'd kept it shut and worked so hard, unknowingly, every single day, to control everything about myself so I could keep control of that door.

I'd been trying to control my appearance, my body, how much food I did or didn't eat, how I presented to the world in terms of clothes and makeup and hair, how I talked, what I said, how I berated myself when I didn't like how I looked or what I said. In other words, my attempts at control turned into dangerously high levels of perfectionism, which then turned into self-loathing anxiety when I inevitably realized how not-perfect I was.

Yet I still thought that if I could control how *close* to perfect I was, then I could control that door and keep it shut. How perfect I could be mirrored how tightly I could hold that door shut.

Everything changed for me when I decided to talk about it. I told my family. I told my best friends. And the more I talked about it, the more I realized it really was a big deal and that I was so, so affected by it.

No more denial. No more minimizing. And that was scary. But the door had been opened—I couldn't shut it even if I wanted to.

I found a holistic therapist who treated my body, my mind, and my connection to Something Greater—the Universe, my Higher Self, Mother Nature, Love, God, Goddess . . . my names for it have changed over the years, but it's all the same.

I slowly began untangling the way the sexual assault had infiltrated itself into every single aspect of my life. It'd all seemed so unconnected—until I really started digging into the root cause for many of my behaviors, thought patterns, and ways I treated myself . . .

It was all due to a rejection of Self. I so deeply

believed I'd done something wrong that night, and that belief had cemented so far within me that I couldn't even begin to glimpse it. "I Am Wrong" and "I Am Bad" were the original beliefs, and the rest of my behaviors and thoughts had been built upon them.

I was living my life, every day, thinking something was wrong with me. So I was never myself. I rejected her, my Self. Because something was wrong with her. And because of that, the deepest layer of the original belief was "I Hate Myself."

To this day, I am still in therapy. It's been three and a half years now since I started openly talking about the sexual assault. The conversation around the assault has lessened over the years, as I've been healing and working through other attempts at understanding myself.

But layers still come up. I still find myself falling into control patterns and perfectionist patterns when I feel shame or vulnerability in new ways. And I am still learning how to cope with each new layer in healthy ways.

But the piece of healing through each layer—what I keep coming back to—is a phrase I was given by Something Greater during a meditative journaling session: "Find beauty in the mystery, and peace in the uncertainty."

So much of our own personal healing is a mystery to us . . . and that is beautiful, if we choose to see it in that way. So much of it is uncertain . . . and we can find peace within that, if we choose to trust ourselves and our Something Greater through each layer we uncover.

Healing is mysterious and uncertain and scary and painful . . . but it doesn't have to be lonely. We can find beauty. We can find peace. We can heal. Together.

Recovery Is Possible!

I didn't think I would live to see age seventeen. I am in my midfifties now. It is a miracle to me that I am not only alive but thriving, thanks to the support of many other survivors of sexual abuse as well as the help of therapy and twelve-step programs.

I was sexually abused by my dad throughout my childhood, from the ages of four to fourteen. The abuse happened mostly in my bedroom at night. My dad would wake me up while I was sleeping and abuse me in my bed.

I became so afraid of going to bed that I would "delay" by getting up repeatedly to talk to my mom. She would eventually get me to stay in bed by giving me a snack to take back to bed with me. That planted the seeds of eating for comfort, which eventually blossomed into an eating disorder later in life.

I wet my bed almost nightly, and my mom would change my sheets in the middle of the night.

She would sing to me while changing my sheets. It was so confusing to be loved and cared for so deeply in some ways, while not at all in other ways. I would wonder why my mom didn't protect me from my dad.

My dad was a scary person filled with so much rage, likely a result of repressing the abuse he'd experienced as a child from his own parents. (My grandfather beat my dad with a Ping-Pong paddle and sexually abused my aunt when she was in a body cast as a young child.) When my parents were first together, my dad used to punch my mom in the stomach when he was upset with her. He switched to kicking her in the shins when she became pregnant with my older sister. He punched holes in closet doors and broke his hand punching a hole in our kitchen wall when I ran away at the age of fourteen.

I became suicidal at the age of ten and started drinking alcohol daily by the time I was twelve. I discovered drugs at fourteen and wound up in treatment for alcohol and drug addiction at the young age of sixteen, after a failed suicide attempt.

I "grew up" attending twelve-step meetings and have thankfully been sober since the age of sixteen. I have spent a lot of time and money on therapy, on surgeries and various treatments and medications for my ailing physical health, and on treatment for an eating disorder.

At the age of twelve, I got down on my knees in the garage and begged my mom to leave my dad. She responded by saying she couldn't possibly leave him. In her own words, "I would be nothing without your father."

I felt hopeless and terrified and so angry. In order to keep myself safe from a psychotic break, I pushed down all the horrible things that happened in my home and pushed down the overwhelming feelings that accompanied them. I drank daily, chain-smoked, became sexually promiscuous with boys and girls, got high, and burned myself with heated-up safety pins. I also began fantasizing regularly about killing myself. By the time I sobered up at sixteen, I had worked so hard to push down the abuse that I had fully suppressed memories of what had happened to me as a child.

My first memories began to surface when my parents separated and ultimately divorced while I was in college. I think the memories began to surface because I felt safer, knowing that my mom wasn't with my dad any longer. I felt really protective of her, despite her inability to protect me as a child. I ultimately came to forgive my mom for her inability to do so. I think the memories also surfaced because I sought out therapy and chose to stop having a relationship with my dad.

Initially, the surfacing of these long-suppressed memories was really overwhelming and confusing.

I felt like I was losing my mind. I would have these flashes of images and emotions that seemed really fragmented and out of context. Sometimes it was just a feeling, like a heavy weight on top of me and difficulty breathing; other times it was a strong scent or sounds. These flashbacks and feelings were always accompanied by intense emotions. I felt like I was a child, back in my bedroom, being abused, having my dad lie on top of me, and being unable to breathe. These sensations felt so real.

Thankfully, I had the support and mentorship of other sexual abuse survivors and a skilled therapist to coach me through these initial memories.

Eventually, I learned to control the memories enough that I could get myself to a safe space, physically and emotionally, before they would fully occur. It was amazing to me that I could actually control the intensity of the memories by "talking" to them. When I felt one coming on, I could say, "Now isn't a good time," or "Let me get to a safe space." For example, I would do this if I felt a memory coming on while driving.

These memories needed to be released, and I learned how to do it at a pace and in a way that ensured my safety and healing rather than retraumatized me. There was a period of a couple of years when the memories really poured out of the place I had buried them. That was an intense time, but I am so glad that I went through it. I occasionally get a new memory now, but the experience isn't nearly as dysregulating because I have developed so many tools to cope with it effectively.

Something that has happened much more slowly is the releasing of shame and self-hate. My self-worth was in the gutter. I believed that I was disgusting and stupid to my core and that my only true worth to the world was sexual. It took a long time to let that go.

I was finally able to release it more completely when I gave up compulsive eating, just a few years ago. The healing that has taken place as a result of giving up this coping mechanism is incredible. I no longer feel shame and no longer live a double life or a life filled with secrecy. I also have so much more self-love and self-compassion. I feel such tender care for the little girl I was, who had been harmed so deeply. I have become her safe, loving, consistent, available, and oh-so-capable parent.

I still have a lot of trauma that resides in my body and expresses itself through migraines and clenching my teeth at night. But I no longer want to hurt myself, let alone end my own life.

Going to bed can feel a little scary when my sense of safety is disrupted—for example, when I am feeling anxious about something at work or feeling stressed for some other reason. I have learned that when I feel scared, I can talk in a soothing, compassionate way to my inner child, or I can meditate, talk to my higher power, and journal.

Today, I experience joy, love, playfulness, and safety on a regular basis. I have created a home and a life with a partner that is safe and filled with love and laughter.

Today, I fully believe that I am a fit, capable, beautiful, competent woman who is worthy of love, of life, and of light.

If I can recover, you can too.

To Tell a Secret

I decided today is the day I begin writing my story. I think back to all the sexual and ritual abuse in my childhood—and after all these years, I still become weepy. I didn't expect that to hit me so quickly.

I think about how the abuse started at age four by my father. I've gone over and over these memories in therapy and with trusted friends through the years, yet they still make an impact. I am surprised, like always, how much they hurt my heart. I remembered a lot of the abuse while growing up and made a conscious decision to block it out or compartmentalize it. It was too much.

When I was a small child, my father was my hero. I used to ride the tractor with him through the fields. I used to watch sports and play football and softball with him. I even got to go to the bar with him and sit next to him on a barstool.

However, I told my mother that my father was sexually abusing me during the times I was with him. My mother told my father. My father severely punished me for telling the truth and threatened worse punishment if I ever told anyone else. I remember a clear thought of how he was going to kill me. I think of this memory now and remember how afraid and alone I felt and the despair of having no one to turn to.

However, I did find someone to turn to, and that was my godmother, Beverly. She listened to all the abuse horror stories. I don't think she knew what to say or what to do. This was a long time ago, when people didn't talk about or get involved in another family's "business." But she would hug me and tell me I was safe with her.

I loved her and her family. They treated me like I was the most important person in the world. She bought the best gifts and took me out for my favorite meal: hamburger and french fries. I knew that whatever I told her, I was safe. I remember how grateful I was to have her, and our relationship lasted for many years.

The sexual and ritual abuse continued for many years, and with each year, it got progressively worse. I found ways to cope. I chose sports and alcohol. I was a great tennis player and pretty good golfer. I started drinking alcohol at age eleven. I came home from babysitting one night and got drunk with my sisters in our basement. I loved it and realized I could forget everything and just be in the moment.

Most of all, I didn't feel the painful feelings I had to deal with on a daily basis.

That worked until age eighteen, when I ended up in rehab. Rehab in the '80s was a lot different than what it is now. Talk about retraumatizing.

The good news is, I had a great counselor who was honest and upfront and saw all the trauma in me. He would periodically ask if my father abused me; I always said no. I didn't want to open that can of worms.

The counselor was able to help me see my own truth about my addiction to alcohol and drugs and how to make peace with it. I left rehab after sixty days and vowed to myself and god that I was never going back. And so far, it's held true. I now have over forty years of sobriety.

Even though the abuse was still happening, my healing started getting stronger when I started going to Alcoholics Anonymous. I had something to hold on to. I loved the meetings and the people in them. The concept of a higher power came easily to me; I took hold and never let go.

I completed a bachelor's degree and earned my master's degree in counseling and psychology. I became a drug and alcohol counselor.

By the time I was in my midtwenties, the compartmentalization of all the memories finally broke. I thought people were hiding in the closet, and I kept hearing voices telling me to kill myself.

The memories started flashing through my mind. I thought I was going crazy. I could barely function, and seeing my own patients was next to impossible.

My psychiatrist had me hospitalized. I was hospitalized four more times after that. The '90s turned out to be a lost decade. I was dealing with the sexual assault and ritual abuse memories. My psychiatrist was trying to stabilize my mental health—to calm the voices in my head and the visual hallucinations.

I was finally diagnosed with severe post-traumatic stress disorder and bipolar disorder. With the help of therapy and medication, the memories slowly became much more manageable. And at last, I was stable.

Around this time, I made the difficult decision to cut off all contact with my family. While it may seem like an easy, no-brainer decision to an outsider, leaving your family—even an abusive one—is difficult.

During this time, I met my first husband, and we married. I knew it was a mistake but felt we could make it. If I had to do it over again, I never would have married him.

Of course, the marriage didn't last, but I knew I would. With medications, Alcoholics Anonymous, therapy, a strong belief in a higher power, and a courage I didn't know I had, I began to get better and stronger.

In 2001, I decided to change my career. I've had psychic gifts since the age of four. I was able to see the future, and I knew what people were going to say before they said it. I could also see angels and spirits around people. This helped protect me from some of the abuse. So I decided to mix the psychic with the psychological. Much to my surprise, the business has been pretty successful. I now have clients all over the United States. I love my work and am so grateful for the god-inspired change.

I married again in 2006. My second husband was from the United Kingdom. Although we had our issues, for the first time in my life, I felt unconditional love and gave it in return. He was truly the love of my life.

The heartbreaking part is that he died in a car accident in 2015. I was devastated and didn't know if I would recover. Those of us who have been abused know grief, but losing a life partner took me to a whole new grief level. Thankfully, my friends, my sister, and a great psychiatrist were all there to pick me up.

A word of caution to those of us who experience grief: don't think the stages of grief go in order; they don't. The best way to make peace with grief and loss is just to keep feeling it and keep working your way through it. My husband has been gone for nearly eight years. I still miss him, but the grief is more manageable. I've made peace with the fact that I will always miss him.

I don't think I'll ever marry again. I've realized that I like my own company and like being with my friends. My relationship with my higher power has gotten even stronger. I meditate every day, which has changed my life.

Today is about living one day at a time. I've also found it's best if I follow a schedule. I've found this keeps me more focused and calmer. I still have memories surface, but instead of feeling devastated, I talk them through and move on. Prayer and meditation also help with the memories.

It's been a long haul to get where I am today, but I realize there are some things you can't rush. You just have to keep marching through it and trust in your own god, resilience, strength, and intuition.

Common Denominator

I was sexually abused from ages six to ten by my step-grandfather. I was then sexually abused by my biological dad from ages ten to fourteen. I had pervasive feelings of being dirty, bad, unlovable, unliked, and at best tolerated.

The traumatic effects were varied and long lasting. I chewed my fingernails and the skin on the side of my nails until I sometimes bled.

I had severe constipation starting at age six; I remember one time not having a bowel movement for eleven days. (More than forty years later, this is still an issue.) I learned to give myself enemas to find relief. It would back up the plumbing when I would finally go, and my mom and stepdad would get upset, as though I'd done it on purpose. It was suggested I go in the woods behind the house. And I did, to avoid their anger.

I ground my teeth so much that I required corrective dental work as an adult. As a teenager,

I had a stomach ulcer and migraine headaches so severe I would throw up.

At times, I had night terrors—a family member would hear the screaming and wake me up. I believed I was trapped in the corner of my room, scratching and banging on the walls, trying to find a way out.

I had immense trouble winding down and being able to fall asleep. And the fact that I couldn't sleep made me worry about my school performance the next day, which made it even harder to relax.

I really started struggling with major depression in my midteens and was medicated by age fifteen. I had extremely intense flashbacks at times and would become terrified—feeling as though I was truly back in an abusive situation.

By age seventeen, I decided life wasn't worth living. I went to say thank you and goodbye to my therapist, who of course hospitalized me. I spent eleven days in a psychiatric hospital, then landed in foster care a month later.

The very first time I breathed a word of the abuse was to my cousin during a sleepover at age ten. She did believe me and suggested I tell my mom. I dismissed her suggestion because of shame and also because my mom was not a safe place for me.

My cousin told her mom (my maternal aunt) after I left, and within a few days, my mom knew. It was reported to authorities, and I was put in counseling. Within months, my step-grandfather spent some jail time.

I finally told my mom directly about the abuse by my dad because I needed a reason why I didn't want to visit him anymore. He was my absolute favorite person on the earth, whom I not only loved but idolized. So my sudden change in attitude toward him was suspect.

My mom believed me, but I think mostly because she hated him and almost seemed to enjoy the fact that he had fallen from the position I held him in. She wondered how the reality of this happening to me *again* would reflect on her. My loss, abuse, and emotions were not acknowledged. It was decided we would ignore the reality of the abuse and just stay away from him.

Sometime later, I requested to go back to counseling because I was really struggling. At that point, the abuse was reported. Ultimately, he spent forty-four months in state prison for first-degree criminal sexual misconduct, along with revictimizing a known victim.

I absolutely believed the abuse was my fault; I was sure somehow I had caused it. And if I hadn't caused it, I hadn't stopped it—I'd gone along with it. So either way, it was my fault. No matter how many therapists or adults told me it was not my fault, I never believed it. I would nod my head in understanding, but deep down, I was filled with shame about my badness.

I was utterly convinced that anyone who truly knew every detail of the situation would blame me as well. Two different, unrelated perpetrators who didn't even know each other and hadn't ever met? What was the common denominator? Me.

I didn't know what it was exactly, but I was inherently bad. And if I couldn't identify it, there was no way I could get rid of whatever it was. Perhaps I could outperform it—make up for it in other ways by being good, achieving, being useful.

It wasn't until my children reached the age when my abuse started that I realized for the first time, "Oh, look at the very young and innocent child—there is absolutely no possible way that the sexual abuse had been my fault. Even *if* I'd initiated or thrown myself at them or cooperated or encouraged it (which I hadn't). There's just *no* way."

I now know that during the abuse from my dad, I was dissociated; it was as though my soul left my body during the events. Although the room was often completely dark, I could "see" myself up in the corner of the room, facing away from what was going on.

I was an achiever. Essentially, I decided not to feel—but to perform. I was going to be a great student and very organized and industrious in all facets of my life.

I struggled with relating to peers. I wanted to

be known, accepted, and understood. But with my story? I knew that wasn't possible. I felt if people really knew me, they would not want anything to do with me. I desperately wanted to connect but felt lonely, isolated, misunderstood.

Maybe the changes in friendships I experienced over the years were typical for any teen, but I felt them much more deeply due to the disconnection with my own family members. I tried to get the love and acceptance from my friends that was not available from my parents.

I have been in therapy on and off since age ten. I bonded really well with my therapists over the years; I felt safe with them and looked up to them. From the time I was fourteen and through young adulthood, I always had a serious, long-term boyfriend. They became my focus, identity, and source of any hope I had.

I was determined to become anything but a product of my environment. I was going to succeed in spite of them. I wanted to prove that their abuse and lack of love and protection were irrelevant. In my mind, success was the best revenge. This was part of my core motivation as early as middle school. I always wanted to heal. I read self-help books as early as junior high and was always interested in and cooperative with therapy. I earned a master's degree in social work and became a therapist—thinking this indeed would heal me.

But performance could not bury it enough. It could not numb out the emptiness, the depression, the lack of feeling truly understood and connected to others, nor the ebb and flow of physical issues (particularly digestion) that were really a result of unresolved trauma. I had no idea at the time how much work there was to do. I thought getting away from my family would be the key, and it was helpful. But I'm glad I did not know in young adulthood that healing literally would be a lifelong endeavor.

Becoming a parent was a huge motivating factor to dive in even deeper and to stay the course, no matter what. I knew all too well what being raised by an unhealed parent was like. I didn't really think I could ever be a *good* parent, but I wanted to do whatever I could to avoid inadvertently injuring my kids due to my own unresolved trauma. At least someday I could recount to them all the efforts I'd made to improve myself, and I could apologize profusely for any way I had fallen short.

I realized that achievements would not heal me—neither would financial status, marital status, nor distance from my family. I had a master's degree, was working in the field of mental health, was on my third marriage, and was living across the country from any relatives. Yet there were still relational issues, triggers, mental health ups and downs, and pervasive feelings of disconnection and shame. I had been in therapy and reading self-help books on and off since middle school, yet here I was, in my thirties, with still so much work ahead of me.

Desperate to not feel anything unpleasant, I've always made working on myself physically a priority. I tried to rid myself of depression, teeth grinding, constipation, stomach ulcers, gallbladder attacks, heartburn, migraines—resolving these was a big driving force in my life. I devoured books on health and alternative medicine and was open to exploring anything I thought would bring not only relief but optimal performance.

Although I didn't fully realize it at the time, I think moving my body has been healing for me. In my twenties and thirties, I did a lot of distance running—from 10Ks to a full marathon. My lifelong dream is to have a strong, muscular body, and I work diligently on that goal today. I think being well physically is part of that desire to not only not *be* a victim but also not *be seen* as one. I also grew up surrounded by obesity and constant comments of "Oh, you just wait"—as though somehow that was my inevitable future.

Currently, I am in my late forties. I can do ten unassisted pull-ups, and I enjoy a variety of hobbies, such as wakesurfing, downhill skiing, and Rollerblading. I understand the value of quality food, and I pay daily attention to nourishing and hydrating myself well. Although this self-care was initiated in sports, I think it has had immense value in indirectly nurturing my younger self, who had not been loved well nor taken care of.

The vast majority of my healing journey involved doing everything I could do to feel nothing. Emotions seemed weak, frivolous, and just simply unnecessary. It wasn't until my forties that I fully realized that emotions are very important cues we receive to help us stay connected to our authentic selves. And having a connected relationship with our authentic selves is critical if we want to have connected, meaningful relationships with others—which I very much desired.

I also realized that my lingering physical issues were related to repressed emotions. So, feeling better physically required a deeper layer of healing and allowing myself to feel and express emotions. I learned that emotions are key in following and knowing my life's purpose and the best, most fulfilling choices for myself. I also learned that emotional numbing was stifling my creativity—another aspect of life that brings joy and fulfillment.

Along with numbing my emotions early on, I also didn't give a lot of thought or credit to the spiritual aspect of life. When I became a mother, I immersed myself as deeply as I could in nondenominational evangelical church culture. To me, this seemed like something a good parent would do, and I desperately wanted to be at least a good enough parent. Small groups, Bible studies, midweek services, Christian school—we did it all over the course of fifteen years.

Ultimately, church culture could take me only so far. As I grew in wisdom and discernment over the years, I realized that the "family of God" I so desperately wanted to be a part of was just another version of dysfunction. It took me far too long to recognize this. True spiritual growth and connection is an ongoing "inside job," and a church body may just be one of the most damaging or distracting elements in that process.

I've been living at the twenty-ninth address of my life for over eighteen years now, and I've been married to my third husband for seventeen of those. We have three kids, and I homeschool them. I have not worked as a therapist since having kids, but I have developed classes I teach to adults and teens that are about creating a healthy, successful, stable life. Health and wellness routines are built into the daily fabric of my life, and I know my adherence to self-care greatly determines my well-being.

It's been only six months since a trigger has pulled the rug out from under me, although those incidences are increasingly rare. During those times, I cut out unnecessary responsibilities, and I add appointments for craniosacral therapy, massage, Reiki, acupuncture, or more frequent coaching until I fully stabilize. I also try to write more, as memories are so raw and accessible. I try to view the situation as an opportunity to work on and heal another layer. And no matter how I feel, I make every effort to stick to my core routines of nutrition, walking, and a regular bedtime, which are vital in helping me return to my normal level of functioning as soon as possible.

In those times, I still have to remind myself that I am not inherently bad; not everything is my fault. My parents' inability to love me well and protect me is a reflection of their brokenness, not my unworthiness.

I would encourage other survivors to *never, never* stop your pursuit of healing. You are a mind, body, and spirit—and each of those facets needs attention and restoration. Your healing will look different at various stages, as it should.

When you're discouraged and considering giving up, keep in mind that abandoning yourself and the hard work of healing will inadvertently hurt the loved ones around you. You deserve the experience of putting forth the optimal version of you, and you want your loved ones to be able to relate to and experience the best of you as well.

Acknowledgments

This book would not exist without the numerous sexual assault survivors who, over many years, were courageous and trusted me with their stories. You all taught me that it was not my shame, it was not my fault, and it is possible to feel safe. I borrowed from your "courage and strength bank" until I was able to trust in my own courage and my own strength. You showed up for me at dinner parties, at family gatherings, at church groups, at alcohol and drug recovery meetings, at the law firm, in books, in magazine and newspaper articles, and in my coaching business. You all continue to help me heal every single day. My gratitude is immeasurable. Together we heal.

This book also would not exist without the constant love, support, and encouragement of my partner in life—my husband, Jon. You've been by my side from the very beginning of my ascent out of the basement. It hasn't been easy for you, but you saw something in me from the very start that I couldn't see. You never doubted me. Thank you.

Thank you to my kids, Ellen and Aaron. Your unending support and unconditional love and forgiveness provide the inspiration I need to keep moving forward.

A very special thank-you to Charlie O., Burnell M., and Mary T. You all saw me before I could see myself. Thank you.

A very special thank-you to Ray Lazar and Bob Zalk, who gave a lost twenty-five-year-old a chance when I really needed one.

Thank you to my fabulous immersion editor, Angela Wiechmann. You are a gift. Your patience with and understanding of my writing style and my slow pace allowed this book to be written. Thank you for never putting pressure on me to "complete" the manuscript. Thank you for trusting and intuitively knowing that this writing process and subject matter were bigger than both of us. You allowed them to unfold.

This book journey experience and completion could not have happened without Ruthie Nelson, the fine-tooth-comb proofreader, and Jay Monroe, the wholly talented artistic designer. Ruthie, your keen eye and placement of a simple comma or colon or dash made all the difference. Jay, your artistic talent to design the book as I envisioned exceeded my expectations. Thank you so much to both of you!

Thank you to my artist, Razieh Alba. You read the first chapter and created the cover art on your first try. Unbelievable. Your art captures the essence of the book. You are gifted and extremely generous with your talent and time. Thank you.

A very special acknowledgment to my beloved sister, Char. You lived it with me, you survived it with me, and we healed together. I thank my God for you.

The final and most important acknowledgment belongs to the God of my understanding—my Spiritual Connection—who is the net that always catches me.

About the Artist

Razieh Alba is an art educator and multimedia visual and conceptual artist drawn to exploring the impacts of trauma and the process of healing. Her work encompasses digital media, sculpture, large-scale art installation projects, and technology to provide immersive experiences that encourage viewers to step away from their own perspectives and potential biases and open themselves up to the stories of trauma survivors.

Throughout her MFA program at the University of Calgary, Alba focused her studies on recovering from trauma related to sexual abuse and the power of moving from the position of *victim* to *survivor.* Part of that process is rooted in the idea of giving testimony to our experiences, where audiences take on the role of witness.

Within the illustrations in *Out of the Basement,* Alba focuses on putting imagery to the struggles of the individual as they move out of the dark and into the light through acts of bravery, community, and the shared experiences of others moving through their own paths toward healing.

RAZALBA.COM

About the Author

Deborah K. Halvorson is passionate about helping people to help themselves. She channels this passion in her life coaching business, Through the Jungle, LLC (throughthejungle.org). She strives to help sexual assault survivors and others focus on creating and experiencing their own well-being while maneuvering through the jungle of life.

Drawing from her profound journey of healing from sexual assaults and addiction, Deb's expertise is deeply personal, underscored by her active role in a recovery program spanning four decades. She knows the courage it takes to face your past and the ever-looming temptation to return to what's familiar, even if it's harmful. The content of this book is based upon those experiences of recovery and healing.

Deb lives in the Minneapolis area and enjoys summers on Lake Carlos.

Further Reading

The author was greatly inspired by the following books:

- *The Power of Now*, Eckhart Tolle
- *A New Earth*, Eckhart Tolle
- *Conversations with God* (series), Neale Donald Walsh
- *The Body Is Not an Apology*, Sonya Renee Taylor
- *Asking For It*, Kate Harding
- *I Know Why the Caged Bird Sings*, Maya Angelou
- *People of the Lie*, M. Scott Peck, MD
- *The Great Work of Your Life*, Stephen Cope

- *Discover the Power Within You*, Eric Butterworth
- *Living Beautifully*, Pema Chödrön
- *The Body Keeps the Score*, Bessel van der Kolk, MD
- *The Book of Joy*, His Holiness the Dalai Lama and Archbishop Desmond Tutu, with Douglas Abrams
- *Change*, Ilchi Lee
- *The Art of Community*, Charles H. Vogl
- *At the Dark End of the Street*, Danielle L. McGuire
- *The Bonobo Sisterhood*, Diane L. Rosenfeld
- *Gentle Power*, Emilia Elisabet Lahti, PhD
- *Trust*, Iyanla Vanzant
- *Outliers*, Malcolm Gladwell